The Future of the Sixth Form

The Future of the Sixth Form

A. D. C. Peterson

Director,
Department of Educational Studies,
University of Oxford

LONDON AND BOSTON
ROUTLEDGE & KEGAN PAUL

First published 1973
by Routledge & Kegan Paul Ltd
Broadway House, 68-74 Carter Lane,
London EC4V 5EL and
9 Park Street,
Boston, Mass. 02108, USA
Printed in Great Britain by
Northumberland Press Ltd
Gateshead
© A. D. C. Peterson, 1973

ISBN 0 7100 7489 1

Library of Congress Catalog Card Number 72-90119

THE STUDENTS LIBRARY OF EDUCATION has been designed to meet the needs of students of Education at Colleges of Education and at University Institutes and Departments. It will also be valuable for practising teachers and education-ists. The series takes full account of the latest developments in teacher-training and of new methods and approaches in education. Separate volumes will provide authoritative and up-to-date accounts of the topics within the major fields of sociology, philosophy and history of education, educational psychology, and method. Care has been taken that specialist topics are treated lucidly and usefully for the non-specialist reader. Altogether, the Students Library of Education will provide a comprehensive introduction and guide to anyone concerned with the study of education, and with educational theory and practice.

The upper secondary school—the sixth form in our usage —is changing as it expands, especially in its social and academic composition. Sixth form studies (which may take place in at least six different kinds of institution) are changing very little. Contrasting with the very wide variety of institutional organisation permitted by our emphasis on local educational freedom, there persists a pattern of upper secondary studies geared to 'O' and 'A' levels that every-one agrees is in need of reform but that the relevant 'partners' in education cannot agree how to reform. In these circumstances, argues Mr Peterson, we must be clear about our purposes in upper secondary education—and get away from some of the myths about the sixth form; then think out what sort of curriculum would enable these objectives to have some chance of realisation; then think of the kind of institution in which such a curriculum might best be followed; and finally, with a rueful regard to the reasons for the failure of previous attempts at reform, decide on how to get the process of change started. In this quietly convincing essay Mr Peterson is a firm re-former, but not in the least insensitive to the fact that we have to take account of the situation as it now is. And his treatment of the problem in England and Wales gains immensely from his detailed knowledge of what is happening in the other countries of Europe and from his association with the successful launching of the International Baccalaureate.

LIONEL ELVIN

Contents

CONTENTS

What is 6ᵗʰ form? 1/3/6 |12| <ins>types</ins> 60 |1|2|3 7 7-1
grammar arms 3/4
reasons ROSLA 7 bigger 6ᵗʰ 8/10
ability of new 6ᵗʰ 11
conclusion 12 |·5| 61-2-3-4-5
6ᵗʰ form work in part ∨ 18|9|21 - A levels/gen subjs
exams- 29 |35|37 | 73-4-5-80

viii

1

The nature of the sixth form

Introduction: definition of the sixth form

Books about the future of anything ought to make at least two things clear on the first page. The first is whether the author is writing about what he thinks the future ought to be or what he thinks it will be. Is he trying to prescribe or to prophesy? The second is what he is writing about.

My answer to the first of these obligations is fairly simple. Primarily this book is concerned to state a view about how education in the sixth form in England and Wales ought to develop. The question of whether it is actually likely to develop in that way will be treated much more briefly in the last chapter.

The answer to the second is much more difficult, certainly more difficult to put on the first page. The term 'sixth form' is becoming more and more ambiguous, as may be seen from the arguments about whether an 'open entry' upper school, accepting all those who elect to remain at school after the age of sixteen, has any right to be called a 'sixth form college'. It is a bad term in an international context since many countries number in a reverse direction to us and the sixième in France is the bottom, not the top, of secondary education.

It is probably a bad term for rational discussion also, because for many people of my generation it is emotionally overloaded. They remember the sixth form as the moment in their youth when, in the company of a handful of others and taught by devoted teachers, they first tasted intellectual excitement and first saw the possibility of entry to a university, with all the accompanying visions of expanded ambitions and upward social mobility. Many of us owe everything to the sixth form and will not forget it. Among such people there will be some who are unlikely to view dispassionately changes in it so radical as to alter its very nature. 'What you are talking about,' they will say, or at least feel, 'may be, in the terms of the Crowther Report, education between fifteen and eighteen, but it is not "The Sixth Form".'

It might have been preferable, therefore, to adopt for this book a neutral title, as the Crowther Report did. But this would hardly have been appropriate since changes in the age range and in institutions are among the things that will have to be discussed.

It seemed better, therefore, to stick to the familiar term, but to make clear at the outset how it is interpreted. By the sixth form, then, I mean the final period of secondary education, not necessarily confined to pupils selected for ability, and occupying, in various European countries, two or three years, somewhere within the age range of fourteen to twenty-one. The earliest entrants to this sixth form are some of the express stream English entering the sixth forms of public schools at fourteen and leaving at seventeen, the latest are the average candidates for the German *Abitur* entering the final two years of the *Gymnasium* at nineteen and leaving at twenty-one. This stage in education is now becoming of crucial importance in most of the developed countries and is in fact a topic chosen for discussion at the 1973 Conference of European Ministers of Education.

The definition accords fairly well with two official definitions of the English sixth form, that of the Schools Council: 'all pupils who stay on at school beyond the academic year in which they reach the age of 16, together with all younger pupils who have begun GCE "A" level courses,' and that of the Department of Education and Science: 'The term Sixth Form should be interpreted as groups of pupils taking courses at a level wholly or mainly beyond GCE "O" level, whether or not the course prepares pupils for the GCE "A" level examinations.'

The reader will notice here a criterion which I have not included in my definition, and a feature of English education to which it will be necessary to revert continually throughout this essay: the nature of the sixth form is defined in both cases by reference to the examinations for which the pupils are preparing. It is perhaps too little realised that England and Wales are the only countries in Europe where the secondary school curriculum is controlled not by any authority, local or central, which has planned it as a curriculum, but by the structure and syllabuses of the public examinations. The virtues and vices of this peculiarity will be discussed in the next two chapters.

Composition of the sixth form

Working on this definition, then, our first question must surely be for whom is sixth form education to be provided. Any attempt to predict this, that is the future composition of the sixth form, must necessarily start from some analysis of its past and present membership. Fortunately, this work has already been done within the present series in A. D. Edwards's *The Changing Sixth Form in the Twentieth Century*. All that is required here, therefore, is the shortest of summaries.

The grammar school sixth form between the wars, like much else in the grammar schools, was the result of a determination by devoted teachers to give the able grammar school pupils the advantages that only the public school had been able to give in the past. It inherited much of the tradition of Arnold's Rugby as modified through the nineteenth century, which is described in David Newsom's *Godliness and Good Learning*. Its pupils were the élite and its successes the pride of the school.

When, at the end of the Second World War, the country committed itself to secondary education for all, there was certainly no thought that this meant anything approaching sixth form education for all. As a former grammar school headmaster, I remember very well right up to 1952, my sixth form of thirty-two pupils and the role it played in a school of over three hundred. It was two years later that the Ministry of Education published their report, *Early Leaving*, which pointed out with alarm that it was unusual for more than one-third of the highly selected pupils of a grammar school (i.e. 6–7 per cent of the age group) to reach the sixth form. The point of take-off had, however, just been reached, with sixth form numbers doubling in the next decade and in the major public schools sometimes outnumbering the rest of the school, a situation of more prefects than fags which would have puzzled Tom Brown.

What is, perhaps, not so generally realised is that England and Wales have been slower than the majority of European countries in this expansion of sixth form education. Table 1, published by the OECD (*Development of Secondary Education*, p. 32) shows the percentage of the seventeen-year-old age group still in attendance at school in the years 1960-5.

Table 1. *Seventeen-year-old age group at school, 1960-5*

	%
USA (1960)	75·6
Netherlands (1961)	44·7
Belgium (1964)	42·2
France (1964)	36·7

Italy (1964)	19·0
W. Germany (1965)	16·9
Portugal (1963)	15·6
England & Wales (1965)	13·7
Denmark (1960-2)	10·0

One of the difficulties of all such comparisons is of course comparability of terminology. It is never quite clear exactly what 'continued attendance at school' may mean, but for England and Wales, at least, the figures were borne out in the survey carried out by the Government Social Survey for the Schools Council in 1967, which remains the most comprehensive and accurate source of information that we have. At that time, of the sixteen- to eighteen-year-old age group, 11 per cent were in school sixth forms and 4 per cent were taking 'full-time non-advanced courses' in the further education sector. This would bring us out for 1967 only just below Portugal's figure for 1963, but still substantially below France, Italy, West Germany and Benelux. Since 1967, there has been continued expansion, and the statistics of education for 1969 reported a substantial increase in school leavers who were aged seventeen or eighteen, in spite of the diminishing size of the relevant age group. The increases were, however, of the order of 9 per cent and 12 per cent and starting from the lower base in a period of general European expansion, it is difficult to estimate how far we are catching up. The 1970 statistics give a figure of 20 per cent of school pupils remaining in school at the age of seventeen. L. C. Taylor, working on the basis of the Department of Education & Science Report no. 51 and a reasonably conservative expansion in further education, concludes that: 'by 1980 we may expect somewhere between 36 and 40 per cent of our sixteen to nineteen year olds to continue with full time education. The Swedes adjusted their national plan to allow for 70 per cent; the French base theirs on 80 per cent' (*Resources for Learning*, p. 32).

5

Already the latest information is that the Swedish figure was an underestimate.

Underlying assumptions of sixth form expansion

Even this rate of expansion of potential sixth formers depends upon three assumptions. The first is that we shall not deny secondary education to those who wish to continue it beyond the statutory leaving age of sixteen; the second is that, despite Ivan Illich, we shall continue to organise education in schools and colleges; and the third is that secondary education will continue to be much less attractive to young people in this country than to those of most other European countries.

The first of these assumptions might be proved wrong. It would be possible for us, if we wished to preserve the sixth form as an academic élite and did not believe in the full-time formal education of the masses beyond a certain stage, to revoke the present regulations by which voluntary staying on at school is allowed and even, to a minimal extent, encouraged, and to require five 'O' levels as a qualification for remaining at a maintained school after the year in which the sixteenth birthday occurred. It is perhaps doubtful whether such a regulation could be imposed on fee-payers in independent schools.

There may be some to whom such a policy would be attractive. It would make it possible to preserve the academic curriculum of the present sixth form with little change; it would save a great deal of money; it could even be seen as a step in the direction of Ivan Illich's 'de-schooling society'.

On the other hand, it is probable that the best career opportunities would still be reserved to those who had remained in full-time education. In that case, by basing continued full-time education not on the commitment of the student but on examination results, we should be placing the burden of determining life-chances on the 'O' level which was once placed on the eleven plus, and which it could not bear; it would mean denying to the average English boy or girl a chance which would be open to those of most other developed countries; and it would surely be tolerable only to the extent that employment in other than dead-end jobs was open to the sixteen year olds who were excluded from school. The fact that it would be 'socially divisive' is placed in neither scale, since those who would support the proposal might well do so because it would produce a more hierarchical society, while those who would oppose it would do so on the same grounds. On balance, therefore, it seems to me neither desirable nor likely that any government—however concerned with the preservation of educational standards—will take this step.

The second assumption, that the increasing numbers of young people continuing their education will spend at least part of it in schools and colleges is also, I think, a safe one.

However valuable the 'de-schooling' attack in such books as *De-schooling Society* or *Compulsory Miseducation* may be in forcing us to reconsider more radically what it is that schools do to their 'inmates', the social effects of a complete abandonment of the institution are too dangerous to contemplate. We do not want the next generation of educators to have to repeat Makarenko's achievement of resocialising the roving bands of displaced children for whom, after the revolution, neither home, school nor work had provided a secure base. This does not, of course, preclude the possibility of a mixture of work experience and school for many in this age group.

On the other hand, it seems both desirable and possible that the third assumption will be proved wrong. By 1973, our statutory leaving age will be as high as any in Europe and the fact that we begin a year earlier will mean that we have the longest period of compulsory education. Why should we continue to have a much lower rate of voluntary staying-on?

To predict the future level of voluntary staying-on is always a hazardous business, but there are a number of factors combining to promote it, not all of which the Department of Education and Science could take into account with any confidence of accuracy in their Report no. 51.

We know, of course, that each raising of the statutory school leaving age has led in the past to a marked increase in the number staying on for the year after that. There is no reason to suppose that when, in 1973, the age goes up from fifteen to sixteen, there will not be the usual increase in the number staying on to seventeen. This is probably the most calculable factor and is included in the estimates already given.

We are less certain of the effects of comprehensive reorganisation. Supporters of the comprehensive school have always maintained that this system would increase voluntary staying-on and the evidence seems to show that they were right. It is much more difficult to guess exactly how much this factor will affect voluntary decisions or at what rate, or which of the many systems will do most to promote it. There are those, for instance, who believe that the sixth form college system, with a break at sixteen would actually discourage staying-on.

Even if this is a false diagnosis, as seems probable, there is not enough evidence yet to justify complete confidence one way or another. It is reasonably safe to assert, however, that comprehensive reorganisation as a whole will accelerate the rise in the staying-on rate, even if it is only a personal opinion that this acceleration is likely to be greater rather than less than is at present anticipated. It is perhaps worth entering a warning here that although reorganisation will increase the size of 'the sixth form' in global terms, certain forms of it will actually diminish the size of individual sixth forms in the short term (see chapter 4).

A third factor is the employment situation. We shall

have to discuss possibilities of mixing sixth form education with employment in chapter 4, but the threat of total
unemployment on leaving school has always been an
inducement to individuals to stay on and to societies to
raise the school leaving age. This was neatly exemplified
by the recommendation of the Institute of Economic
Affairs in December 1971 that the Government should
bring forward the raising of the school leaving age in
view of the high level of unemployment. The strong
adverse reaction to this of the National Union of Teachers
was understandable, in so far as the proposal took no
account of the educational planning involved. The suggestion that educational decisions should not be influenced
by changes in the social and economic situation was unrealistic.

This factor is even more difficult to predict, since it
depends on the economic structure and patterns of employment in the country as a whole. In theory, no doubt,
the search for higher productivity per man-hour, coupled
with higher wages and ultimately, automation in primary
production, should lead to a rapid shift to service occupa-
tions, a shortening of hours and a demand for a more
generally educated labour force. Most educational planning in developed countries is based on such assumptions
and in macro-economic terms, the assumptions are, no
doubt, justified. But in the short term and in individual
areas, the process seems to lead to a great deal of dis-
location in personal lives and periods of very considerable
unemployment. In such circumstances, organised labour
is likely to exert considerable pressure to keep teenagers
off the labour market.

Daniel P. Moynihan, the then Assistant Secretary of
Labor in the USA and subsequently the President's adviser
on urban affairs, in a paper given at a symposium on
universal higher education in 1965, supported a great
expansion in the college population on the grounds that
the addition of one million new students 'would release

an average of 400,000 jobs annually over the decade, which could be occupied by other unemployed in the labor force' and that they would also create another 300,000 jobs, of which 150,000 would be permanent, on the campuses (E. J. McGrath, *Universal Higher Education*, p. 75).

How far our kind of society will move in the direction of seeing unemployment as a great social as well as an economic evil and the creation of jobs as good in itself, is not for educators to predict. It does seem probable, however, that as long as jobs are in short supply, there will be a growing pressure to keep teenagers out of them. Nor do I find it easy myself to imagine exactly what job the sixteen- to eighteen-year-olds could usefully be filling in the expanding service industries, other than some form of trainee apprenticeships (see chapter 4). The only safe conclusion seems to be that the threat of unemployment on the one hand and the demand for a more generally educated work force on the other, will be additional factors pushing up the rate of voluntary staying-on.

My own estimates would be, therefore, that even assuming that the pattern of education did not change very much, the proportion of the sixteen- to eighteen-year-old age group choosing to continue their education might rise to 45–50 per cent by the end of the seventies. It is, of course, already well above that figure in certain areas of England and Wales. But surely it is a very pessimistic assumption that the pattern of education will not greatly change.

Educational implications of the expanded sixth form

This increase in numbers would inevitably bring with it profound changes in the abilities and interests of sixth formers and such changes ought to impose changes in the education provided. The whole teaching programme and social organisation of the sixth form in the past has been based on the assumption (already falsified some years ago) that the majority of them are going on to university education and that they still form a comparatively small élite group which 'gives tone to', 'sets standards for' and generally controls, through the prefectorial system, the rest of the school. It assumes, too, that the sixth form represents the top 15–20 per cent of the ability range, ability being measured by the capacity to pass examinations.

The concept of the 'new sixth form' is of course familiar by now to educational planners. The pamphlet issued by the Head Masters Association in 1968, *The Sixth Form of the Future*, recognises the kind of change which is already in progress. I want to suggest, however, that the scale and speed of the change may be even greater than has been anticipated, simply because the measures which we shall be forced, and quite rightly forced, to take to accommodate 'new sixth formers' on the scale which is anticipated, will so change the nature of sixth form education as to remove many of those inhibitions which at present restrict voluntary entry to it at so low a level. The expansion of the sixth form will thus bring about changes that make it more attractive to those who at present do not seek to enter it. The growth rate will then become exponential and, unless we deliberately restrict entry, we shall find sooner than we expected that completion of the sixth form course is the normal expectation of the great majority of pupils.

One further factor needs to be borne in mind when forming this mental picture of the membership of the sixth form of the future. Because we are in the habit of measuring ability by I.Q. tests or, more often at this stage, academic examinations of a particular type, it is easy to assume that the ability range in the new sixth form will be much wider, but measured along the same single scale as at present.

All our experience of practical life assures us that ability to do well at 'O' level is not by any means the only form of ability that counts. Indeed, some readers will probably remember a cartoon showing a British car inextricably involved in an infuriated snarl of French traffic, while father turns to son with the pregnant words: 'Now then, "O" level French, this is your big chance.'

If we do not restrict the sixth form to those of good 'O' level ability taking 'post-"O" level' courses, but attract into it higher proportions of the age group by offering them courses which seem to them worth staying on for, then we shall find in the sixth form not just a wider range of ability along the familiar 'O' and 'A' level scale, but a greater diversity of abilities. It is the provision of an education suitable for this much more numerous, but also more diverse clientele that the following chapters attempt to discuss.

It will, I hope, become clear that the elements in it cannot usefully be discussed in isolation. It was a step in the right direction when the Schools Council combined for the first time responsibility for curriculum and examinations; but a realistic approach requires that these two be considered in relation to teaching methods on the one hand and institutions on the other.

It is when one looks at the institutions as well as the curriculum and examinations of the sixth form that one is most clearly driven to the urgent need for yet one more advisory committee, or even perhaps a Royal Commission, to bring order out of the chaos which is threatening this most important sector of our education.

It would be not unnatural for those who care for educational reform and have lived through the aftermath of Robbins, Crowther, Newsom, Plowden and James to greet such a suggestion with dismay. We do not surely want more delay, more discussion, more acres of appendices, more embittered controversy on the merits of the proposals, ending in disagreements, exhaustion and disillusion while the mice nibble away at the dusty pages?

I hope to suggest in chapter 5 some changes in procedure which might avoid this dreary outcome. Meanwhile the following pages might be considered as 'personal evidence in writing' to a Royal Commission which may never be set up.

2

The objectives of sixth form education

The content of sixth form education: determination
of objectives

In trying to decide what kind of educational experience
we should provide for this proportion of our youth, we
have to take into account more factors than seem usually
to be considered.

Since the publication of Bloom's *Taxonomy of Educational Objectives*, it has become fashionable to approach
the problem of curriculum development from this point of
view. We must analyse our objectives, we are told, break
them down into specific cognitive or affective goals and
describe them in operational terms. Only then shall we
be able to determine whether the educational experiences
we are providing are well calculated to produce the desired
results and to measure validly and reliably the extent to
which they are doing so.

All this, of course, is partially true. But as a rationale
for judging an existing curriculum or planning a new one,
it is less than half of the truth. 'We' in such statements
are rather like the mysterious and godlike 'we' in Plato's
Republic. What of 'them', the pupils, and their objectives?
Are they to have no say in the content of their education?

Tolstoy wrote in his *Pedagogical Essays*:

> The need for education lies in every man; the people love and seek education as they love and seek the air for breathing; the government and society burn with the desire to educate the masses and yet, notwithstanding all the force of cunning and the persistence of governments, the masses constantly manifest their dissatisfaction with the education which is offered them and step by step submit only to force.

Many educational planners in the Western world are beginning to find how true this is of the late adolescent or almost mature young person, that is of the sixth former, compelled either by laws or by social and economic pressure to remain in an institution called a school and to perform a series of operations called 'lessons'. One does not need to be a committed disciple of Ivan Illich to realise that any attempt to design the right sort of curriculum for the sixth form must take into account their objectives as well as ours. We all sneer at the 'little pitcher filling' model of education, but filling little pitchers with nicely calculated dollops of experience may become almost as counter-productive as filling them with standardised dollops of information.

Yet even this is not enough. Teachers form an integral part of every sixth form and teachers' objectives may be different from either theirs or ours; and if there is one lesson which educational reformers ought to have learnt by now it is that no educational reform is worth the paper it is written on unless the teachers are either ready or can be persuaded to accept and implement it. This may not be easy. All professions tend to resist change and teachers in all countries are, for reasons which I have tried to analyse elsewhere (*The Future of Education*, ch. VII), even more conservative than most professions. I have suggested also that there are special reasons why in our own context headmasters and senior sixth form masters are likely to be more alarmed by proposals for change in the sixth form than in any other area of education under their control.

How else can one account for the extraordinary way in which the sixth form curriculum in this country has survived unchanged in spite of all the changes around it, and for the persistence of the defensive myths by which, in spite of all the evidence, this survival has been justified? Since the sixth form curriculum, whatever may be our or their objectives, is going to be taught or managed for many years to come by those who are at present teaching in it, it would be quite unrealistic to discuss what it ought to be and perhaps will be, without examining first what it is and why those ultimately responsible for it have kept it so long unchanged. In order to do so, we must examine the degree to which the myths represent the reality. These myths are of three kinds, myths about our objectives, myths about their objectives and myths about what actually happens. Let us consider first the myths about what actually happens, since myths of the other two kinds may well be unconscious defence mechanisms called into play to justify the maintenance of existing practice.

The myths of the curriculum: myths about facts

In all European countries, of course, there is a certain degree of difference between the rosy-hued myth of what the best teachers agree ought to be happening in school lessons and the actual experience of the average pupil. Only in England and Wales is there a myth about what lessons actually take place. This is because these are the only countries where the structure of the sixth form curriculum is not prescribed by some central or provincial authority. While in France, Germany or even super-liberal Sweden there may be many different 'tracks' which a sixth former may choose between, the pattern of each track has been established by a controlling authority and it is easy to know what it is. In this country, if you want to know what subjects sixth formers are studying or can choose between, and for how many periods a week they study them, you have two alternatives.

Either you can gather a group of eminent headmasters and other educationists together in a committee and ask them, or you can conduct a survey. The objection to the first course is that the people you ask cannot really know the answer. They know what goes on in their own school and perhaps in one or two others, but they cannot possibly know what goes on in all schools or in the average school. Because they are eminent, the schools with which they are familiar are probably the best schools and this is one of the causes of the myth, which consists largely of the assumption that what happens in the best schools happens in most schools. The objection to the second course is that surveys are very expensive and they take so long to carry out and process, that they always tell us not what is happening in the schools now, but what was happening two or three years ago. Nevertheless it is my contention that on a factual matter like this the results of surveys are much more likely to get near the truth and the committees of eminent men to subscribe to a myth than vice versa, and that, since over the last fifteen years the results of surveys and the opinions of committees have differed consistently and in the same direction, myth-making has been going on somewhere and probably in the committees.

The area of factual disagreement has been, and is, the familiar one of the degree of specialisation. The myth has two features, a purely factual one and an evaluative one. The factual one is concerned with time allocation and is that 'non-specialist' work, that is work not connected with the two or three subjects which he is preparing for GCE 'A' level, occupies one-quarter to one-third of the sixth former's working time. The evaluative one is that it forms an important part of his education.

Let us now turn to the evidence, taking first the opinions of eminent men and contrasting them with the findings of surveys. In 1959 the Crowther Report stated (p. 257) of the sixth form that

> boys and girls spend *up to* [my italics] three quarters of their time (if private study in school hours is included) in their last two or three years at school on a range of subjects which for many of them is a little, but not much, wider than that on which they will spend the next three years as undergraduates if they go to a university. The remainder of their time, which we describe in this report as 'minority time' is normally divided between a number of subjects etc.

Clearly these eminent men believed the myth regarding a time allocation of one quarter as the *minimum* that non-specialised work was getting; but they also considered that it was 'often neglected and wasted' though 'of vital importance' (p. 282).

It was the publication of the Crowther Report which really started the dispute which has been going on ever since and this is, therefore, an appropriate moment at which to clarify terminology as well as to point out the conflict between the evidence of committees and that of surveys. The first survey, financed by the Gulbenkian Foundation and carried out in the same year, 1959, by the Oxford University Department of Education, was based on a stratified random sample of 117 sixth forms. It indicated that the average sixth former's weekly work load consisted of thirty-five three-quarter-hour periods and between eighteen and twenty hours of homework (rather more than the findings of the Linstead Report which was an average of fifteen and a half hours). A varying number of the thirty-five periods were given to private study. Both homework and private study were devoted overwhelmingly to work for 'A' level subjects.

A rational discussion of the proportion of time devoted

by sixth formers to specialised as opposed to non-special-ised work ought clearly to have included homework in the total work load. We are constantly told that the sixth form prepares pupils to work on their own at the university and, in that context, to treat homework as if it did not exist or did not matter made no sense. To have included it, however, would have made obvious nonsense of the myth that general as opposed to specialised studies occupied one-third to one-quarter of the sixth former's time. In fact the argument has always been carried on on the assumption that homework does not count. Its ex-clusion may perhaps have been due to an unconscious determination to preserve the myth. Including homework, the Oxford survey found that nine-tenths of the work load went to specialist subjects and even excluding home-work, six-sevenths (*Arts and Science Sides in the Sixth Form*, p. 6). This was the first conflict of evidence between committees and surveys.

Private study has affected the calculation only because in the early days, some of those most anxious to preserve the myth, at least as far as the daily timetable went, did so by calculating the number of *contact* periods devoted to 'A' level subjects, deducting these from the total number of periods in the week, and then making the quite un-warrantable assumption that the remainder of the time was devoted to general studies. Finally, there have been some difficulties over terminology in deciding whether periods given to subjects from which pupils normally have a right to withdraw, such as religious education and games should be automatically included in the general studies proportion. I once had a student who claimed that she had done *nothing* in the sixth form but physics and mathematics and when I expressed disbelief replied, 'Oh yes, the science sixth did have one period of R.I. and two of English, but I was excused those because I was working for a Cambridge scholarship.'

These confusions in terminology and method have

usually been eliminated from the most recent discussions, but may still underlie some of the opinions of eminent men and generalisations drawn from earlier 'factual' descriptions.

The Crowther Report, even if it was at variance with the survey on the factual part of the myth, did at least question the validity of the myth on its evaluative side.

This position was reversed, however, by the next eminent committee report, that of the Secondary Schools Examination Council in 1962 which roundly stated: 'We do not agree that general studies now occupy in the sixth a lowly and ineffective place' (*Sixth Report of the SSEC*, para. 9). On what evidence they came to this conclusion has never been revealed. It is certainly in conflict with two surveys carried out in the same year. One which involved over one thousand freshmen entering the University of Oxford in 1962, divided into eight separate categories, showed that the average proportion of the weekly timetable devoted to non 'A' level work was 16 per cent and in no category more than 20 per cent. Whether this was 'lowly' or not, it was considerably less than the 'one quarter to one third' which the myth maintained (*Oxford Magazine*, February 1964).

It may be objected that Oxford entrants were an unrepresentative and particularly specialised group, but to some extent at least, they represented the practice of their schools and not merely the experience of individuals. The other survey was that carried out by A. H. Iliffe (1966) on entrants to the University of Keele. This was perhaps more concerned with 'effectiveness' than 'lowliness', but its finding, that 'the accounts which students give of their general studies courses were overwhelmingly critical. It is clear that the most frequently mentioned failings spring directly from the low prestige which is attached to courses of this kind' (*The Foundation Year at Keele*) hardly squared with the opinion of the eminent committee members of the SSEC.

Both the myth and the debate continued, apparently unconcerned at this conflict of evidence, until in 1967, the Schools Council commissioned a totally impartial body, the Government Social Survey, to find out what was really happening. The three volumes of their report were not available until 1970, but are still the most reliable evidence we have (*Sixth Form Pupils and Teachers*, vol. I of the survey carried out for the Schools Council by the Government Social Survey).

On the factual part of the myth, they reported that 47 per cent of sixth formers were taking little in the way of general studies except physical training (including games) and religious instruction and that this occupied less than one-fifth of their timetable and presumably none of their homework. Of the other half of sixth formers, another third were spending less than one-quarter of their time-tabled time on non-specialist work and only one-tenth were approaching one-third of the time (*Sixth Form Pupils and Teachers*, p. 187).

One might have thought that in these conditions it would have been impossible for the committees of eminent men to continue to believe that the average sixth former devoted 'between one-quarter and one-third' of his time to non-specialist work. Yet in 1968 the Head Masters Association published a report, *The Sixth Form of the Future*, which described the normal curriculum thus (p. 13):

> As in the majority of schools today his study in depth would occupy no more than two thirds of his weekly time-table, and the principal element of his work in minority time would be his General Studies programme, covering a wide range of topics and activities according to the particular interests of the staff, the needs of the pupils and the resources of the school.

Are not the only reasonable conclusions to be drawn from this long history of discrepancy that, since the committees never produce any evidence for their views, we should be wiser to trust the surveys than the committees? and perhaps that the vitality of the myth in the face of all evidence to the contrary indicates an emotional commitment to the protection of some loved but threatened illusion?

The myths of the curriculum: myths about teacher objectives

The myth about our own objectives, by which I mean the objectives of those actually engaged in determining the education of the sixth former, has also been in conflict with the realities. It has been pointed out again and again that what universities say, which is that they want broadly educated sixth formers, conflicts with what they actually do, which is to allot the coveted places to those who do best in their specialist subjects, irrespective of their general education. But it is not only universities which are open to this accusation of bad faith or unconscious deception.

The Government Social Survey asked both teachers and pupils in sixth forms to state their 'objectives' for sixth form education. Paragraph 355 and Table 101 place in rank order thirty-one different sixth form objectives for the 'academic' and the 'less academic' pupil, as seen by teachers and pupils. The objectives vary from 'ensuring that all pupils can express themselves orally with ease', rated eleventh by both types of pupil and ninth for 'academic', sixth for 'less academic' by teachers, to 'giving them an opportunity to participate in community service' rated twenty-ninth by both types of pupil but rather higher by teachers. 'Giving them a very thorough knowledge of two or three subjects only' is rated by teachers twenty-ninth and thirty-first, and by pupils thirtieth and thirty-first.

Turning back to paragraph 217, we find that the average sixth former spent thirty periods a week on examination work, to say nothing of twelve or thirteen hours of home-work (see Table 85) and less than nine periods a week on general studies or unexamined work. What were those forty hours or so per week giving him if not 'a very thorough knowledge of two or three subjects only'? They may, of course, have been helping him to 'read and study on his own', ranked first among objectives for academic pupils, but were they really contributing to the following objectives, all ranked even for 'academic' pupils above the 'very thorough knowledge of two or three subjects only': 'giving them information about the courses of further and higher education open to them' (second), 'ensuring that they can express themselves clearly in writing' (third), 'helping them to develop their personalities and characters' (fourth), 'encouraging them to develop a considerate atti-tude towards other people' (tenth), 'helping them to de-velop an interest in subjects other than those studied for examinations' (seventeenth).

How does it come about that teachers and pupils put bottom of their list the objective which 'A' level examiners are mainly concerned to test and which appears, on the allocation of time devoted to it, to be at least the main purpose of the sixth form curriculum?

A similar contradiction arises when one examines the objectives of teachers of arts subjects (para. 433). Top of the list comes 'arousing the pupil's interest in and en-thusiasm for the subject'. Yet the 'A' level examiners do not attempt to measure how far this objective has been achieved, and the form of the examinations, and therefore of the teaching, is hardly designed to achieve it. Does any-one believe, for instance, that concentration on a very thorough knowledge of a limited number of set books is the best way to arouse a pupil's interest in and enthusiasm for English literature? And what about the second most important objective on the list, 'to encourage pupils to read widely'? Are teachers really not familiar with the objection, 'But, sir, it's not on the syllabus'? And if they

are, are they really powerless, if this is what they genuinely feel about objectives, to alter the syllabus? The
International Baccalaureate syllabus for Language A at
a higher level requires considerably wider reading than
'A' level English although it is part of a much wider sixth
form course; but it does not require replies to examination
questions testing detailed knowledge of the 'set books'.

Fourth on the list, amazing as it may seem, comes 'to
ensure that pupils are aware of aspects of the subject
beyond those which are in the examination syllabus.'

Perhaps the best way to compare these statements of
objectives with actual practice is by looking at the *Guide
to the Sixth Form*, quoted in the next chapter.

Yet another contrast is that three-quarters of sixth form
teachers considered (in 1967) that some of their pupils
would be better suited to courses other than 'A' levels, but
even now, five years later, no such courses exist within
the dominating examination system.

Is the contrast between stated objectives and actual
practice then due to the fact that teachers were stating
their personal objectives but neglecting to explain that they
were prevented from actualising them by the demands of
the examining boards? In one respect this may be so. Only
one-third of teachers considered 'that the syllabus allowed
ample time for pursuing fruitful ideas and topics which
were outside its strict bounds'. In general, however, 70 per
cent of teachers were 'satisfied on the whole' with the
syllabuses provided by the boards. The difficulty in
interpreting this of course lies in the words 'on the whole':
only 5 per cent were 'completely satisfied', and what
degree of dissatisfaction was compatible with 'satisfied on
the whole' as opposed to 'dissatisfied on the whole' is hard
to assess. At least the figure 'satisfied on the whole', 70
per cent, was much higher than that of 'dissatisfied on the
whole', 22 per cent.

Yet another contradiction is between paragraph 470
where 92 per cent of all teachers 'considered General

Studies a valuable part of the Sixth Form curriculum' and paragraph 220, which revealed that nearly half of all sixth formers (47 per cent) were 'taking little in the way of general studies except physical training (including games) and religious instruction'. If the 92 per cent think they are valuable, why cannot they ensure that the pupils get them? Or perhaps each individual believes that in other schools than his own, the Head Masters Association's claim was true and that general studies occupied one-third of the sixth former's time.

Surely again the only conclusion to which one can reasonably come is that there is a wide divergence between the myth and the fact of our own objectives as controllers of sixth form education.

The myths of the curriculum: myths about pupil objectives

The myth about *their* objectives started thirteen years ago in the Crowther Report with what I have analysed elsewhere as 'the Myth of Subject-Mindedness' (*Universities Quarterly*, June 1960). It might be thought cantankerous to continue to tease this unfortunate concept, which is now referred to in the James Report (*Teacher Education and Training*, p. 24) as 'a trap', were it not for the fact that it was the sole justification produced in the report for a unique pattern of specialisation in the sixth form which seems to have changed little, and that only in the direction of becoming more rather than less intense (cf. Government Social Survey Report), in the succeeding years.

The theory, as expounded by the Report, was that 'the mark of a good and keen sixth former' was 'a special devotion to a particular branch of study' (para. 333), 'a readiness and eagerness to get down to the serious study of some one aspect of human knowledge which, with the one-sided enthusiasm of the young, they allow for a time to obscure all other fields of endeavour' (para. 387). This subject-mindedness the report considered to be 'a great emotional impulse', 'there, whether we use it or not', in fact, a constant factor in adolescence. It is true that we find later on that this great emotional impulse arises only in the 'ablest' 6 per cent of the population who are going to universities and that it arises at whatever age they enter the sixth form. Even in 1959, it did not apparently arise in girls who were going to what were then teacher training colleges. I can well remember the peals of happy laughter which I used to evoke from sixth formers merely by reading to them the description of themselves and their presumed objectives from the pages of the Report.

It would be easy to dismiss as irrelevant this farrago of special pleading disguised as psychology, for which no evidence was ever produced, on the grounds that the committee itself regarded it as applying only to a 6 per cent minority, already less than one-third and soon likely to be less than one-fifth of the sixth form population; but since the only theoretical basis for what is actually happening not just to the top 6 per cent, but to sixth formers as a whole, is this myth about their own objectives, we cannot dismiss it so lightly.

Like most myths, it was not the cause of a ritual but invented to explain a ritual. The ritual has its origins far back in the history of the sixth form with the defence by Thring of education 'in one noble subject', the classics, against the threat posed by science, modern languages and social studies. Because England, alone in Europe, had no Ministry of Education to settle the feud between Ancients and Moderns and to impose a balanced curriculum of general education, the war was settled by partition, the classical, science and modern sixth each staking out its own territory and excluding the enemy. Their exclusivity was encouraged by the universities in practice, though deplored in theory. Since there were always more qualified applicants than places in universities, competition for them, and for Oxbridge scholarships, became intense, and since admission was decided not by the University but by the Faculty, this competition operated in terms of the specialist subject concerned, the 'one aspect of human knowledge'. In such circumstances, it was inevitable that pupils would be driven more and more by ambition, and schools by the prestige which university scholarships or places conferred, to concentrate on the specialised field of knowledge which paid off in the competition. The best teachers, themselves over-specialised in their own education (I have heard a physics graduate protest that he could not be expected to teach chemistry to twelve-year-olds), made of their specialised courses in the best schools something intellectually exciting; the best pupils responded to this; and so, partly out of need to explain the ritual to which we had become accustomed and partly by generalising from the rare best experience, the myth was born.

It is important to remember that it is concerned not with the pattern of education which sixth formers ought to have, but with the pattern for which they themselves feel a deep emotional need. The English sixth form pattern of early and almost exclusive specialisation in a narrow homogeneous range of studies was presented as profoundly 'child-centred'.

Under the combined influence of surveys and of the expansion of the sixth form to take in 'new sixth formers' in whom 'subject-mindedness' was not to be expected, overt adherence to the myth has largely declined and the word is out of fashion. I shall suggest in chapter 5, however, that covert adherence to it still lives on and is largely responsible for the failure of every attempt to change the sixth form curriculum since the publication of the Crowther Report. It is worth recording, therefore, some of the evidence.

For the deep emotional impulse there is no evidence except the opinion of the eminent men who had observed it. Against, we have the fact that it does not appear to operate outside England and Wales, which is strange if

27

it is a natural feature of adolescence, and that it is confined to such a strictly limited proportion of the age group, identified not by any psychological characteristics but by 'ability' (to pass examinations) and academic intentions (i.e. entry to universities rather than colleges of education).

Nor does the survey evidence support the myth. The Gulbenkian Report, based on the contemporary 6 per cent sample, found that 62 per cent of boys were indeed taking either three or four science 'A' levels which might have looked like 'subject-mindedness', but that when asked which subjects they would have taken, had it not been for university entrance requirements, half replied that they would have dropped one of their science subjects in favour of an arts subject. The Government Social Survey produces two responses which seem at first sight incompatible. When asked to rate the degree to which they liked the 'A' level subjects they were doing with a rating of 1 representing 'I like the subject so much that I would study it even if I did not expect it to be of any use to me', 75 per cent of all assessments got a 'liking rate' of 1 or 2. On the other hand 36 per cent of those taking only science 'A' levels and 29 per cent of those taking only arts 'A' levels replied that they would have liked to be studying a mixture of arts and science subjects (para. 192). Since the number who actually were taking this very 'unsubject-minded' mixture had by then risen to 10 per cent, or if one includes science mixed with social science, 14 per cent, a reasonable estimate would be that in 1967, something between 35 and 40 per cent of all sixth formers either were taking or wanted to take mixed arts and science courses, even within the tight limits of a three 'A' level programme. If one considers all the pressures working in favour of commitment to one side or the other, one is driven to the conclusion that in them at least, the deep emotional impulse was working the other way.

It is never wise to be too dogmatic about pupils' preferences and important as *their* objectives are, they should not surely override ours completely. The safest conclusion to come to is surely that subject-mindedness is not as widespread or as deeply emotional a condition as Crowther supposed, and that belief in the myth may represent a falsification of the pupils' objectives in order to bring them into greater conformity with those of the teacher. If this, or something like it is so, there is no need to distort our objectives for sixth form education in order not to thwart a deep emotional impulse which may not exist or may exist very rarely.

It could be very reasonably argued that this distortion has persisted because of another myth, in this case perhaps an unconscious one, that the great majority of sixth formers are bound for higher education in universities. Certainly it is the pre-university course which has attracted most of the attention. Although there has been a great deal of concern with the 'new sixth former', it is the problems of the 'old sixth former' which have attracted most of the detailed attention.

One danger of this process is that the long series of failures to reach any agreement on reform of the old pre-university curriculum is leading to the view that the curriculum for the new terminal group should be quite separate. Since we seem driven to mark off all educational divisions in this country by means of examination systems, this would require the introduction of yet another public examination, the Certificate of Extended Education, as an alternative in the sixth form to 'A' level.

It is strange that we have not learnt from the bitter experience of trying to divide our pupils into 'O' level streams and CSE streams to avoid this kind of division. How are we to tell, with the constantly expanding opportunities in higher education, which of our sixth formers are pre-university and which are not? The evidence of the social survey shows pretty clearly that there have always been more who see themselves as bound for higher education than actually get there. And who is to deny them the chance? Moreover, our experience of comprehensive education in the earlier stages of secondary education might lead us to conclude that it is worth preserving as long as possible at least some sort of contact between the future intellectuals and the rest of society.

Objectives for the new sixth form curriculum

Do we not need, therefore, to work out some sort of programme for this age group, or at least half of it, which meets their needs as persons as well as developing their intellectual powers as 'scholars', and which, by postponing as long as possible intellectual commitments and irrevocable exclusions, preserves both social harmony and the possibility of individual development?

What then will sixth formers, of both types, ultimately perhaps all young people between the ages of fifteen and seventeen or eighteen, need from education? And since it is their objectives as well as ours that we must consider, what do they want?

We should not, I suggest, look at this stage as either terminal or preparatory, but as a phase in a continuous process of life-long education. How far that process is formally organised and how far simply lived through, like the old 'university of hard knocks', will vary for different individuals in different societies. Our business is to do the best we can for everybody with the resources and within the restraints that our society currently provides.

In these terms, every sixth former, whether in school or out of it, needs and wants to develop his capacity for interpreting his environment, for understanding life. This means not only his external environment, the social and to a lesser extent the physical and technological environment in which he lives, but the inner environment of his own personality. This, for the great majority, takes precedence over purely intellectual curiosity. 'What sort of a person am I?', 'Where am I going?', 'Is this a just society?', 'Is there a God?', are surely more important questions for the average sixth former than 'what is the mathematical structure of the physical universe?' or 'how do historians establish historical truth?'

We are much concerned, and rightly, with the achievement of freedom in our complex, highly organised society, but it remains true that to know the truth is the road to freedom. Rousseau, the most perceptive of all 'educationists', was baffled by the conflict between freedom and reason, but at least he saw and felt it deeply. If our sixth formers are to be free as youths and grow into free men, we must help them to get as much understanding of their total environment as they can and we must encourage them to regard understanding as an important element in choice. The dangers of conditioned choice, as opposed to free choice, may be greater in a democratic society, which is striving to become an educated society, than they have been in formal hierarchic societies, simply because of the hidden nature of the conditioning agents and the social controls.

But the young do not merely want and need to understand their environment, they want to operate within it, they want to be able, in some respects at least, to be able to change it. One does not need to adopt a Marxist epistemology to realise that, at least in this stage of education, knowledge, for the majority, derives from operation. Quite as important as existential questions about the nature of the self and the universe are operational questions—such as: 'Shall I ever be able to hold down a job?' or 'shall I ever be able to bear and look after a baby?' Reassurance about competence is important to the adolescent as well as reassurance about identity. Education must therefore be concerned with that sort of knowledge which is directed towards what Bacon called 'operation' as well as 'satisfaction'.

Two objectives of sixth form education acceptable both to 'us', that is society, and to 'them', the pupils, are therefore:

(a) to enable the student to understand better, and to the best of his ability, both now and as he grows older, himself and his environment,

(b) to enable the student, both now and as he grows older to operate within and upon his environment

These may sound objectives of a very high degree of abstraction and certainly not very Bloomian; but they do give rise to a number of practical corollaries which will be developed in the next chapter. At least it should be clear that they imply the development of the powers of the mind, rather than the transmission and storing of information for its own sake, that this development should be general, covering the whole range of conceptualisation and methodology through which we interpret our experience; that this general development should be linked to practical operation rather than purely to abstract reasoning; and that it should be accompanied by the development of his ability to communicate with his fellow men. These principles alone would lead to a sixth form education very different from that which at present exists.

But education should surely do more than teach a man to understand and to modify his environment. The end of all education is the increase of human happiness. Man seeks, and Christians believe that he is meant to seek, to enjoy his world, as well as to understand and change it. Education for enjoyment of the world, again perhaps, as in the case of understanding, both passive and active, should surely form a substantial part of sixth form education.

Such a trio of objectives would imply a general education which provided educative experience in what Professor Hirst has called the different fields and disciplines which make up our consciousness of ourselves as active in our environment. It should not be thought of as pre-paratory, that is simply as developing the students' capacity to think, to operate or to enjoy, but as active and creative, as developing these powers by using them here and now. It should not therefore be isolated in a school or in a range of school subjects which belong in schools and no-where else. It should be relevant, not because this is what trend-conscious students demand, like those in California who demanded that all university courses should be re-structured to take account of the invasion of Cambodia, but because this is what educates. Nor should we forget that relevance means not only what we consider to be relevant to their future needs, like learning the essential structure of a foreign language, though this is important, but also what they feel to be relevant to their present needs, like learning to communicate with and relate to other people.

Finally, there is a synthesising objective which seems to me appropriate, but which many, particularly perhaps among the young, may find much harder to accept. This is that it should strive to develop among students an acceptance, at the most fundamental level, of the kind of society in which we live. This most emphatically does not mean acceptance of all the features in it or all its values. But a society is an organic body. Only those who, at the deepest level, remain within it and accept it as having value and the potential, with however radical reform, of even greater value, can operate within it and seek to improve some parts of it, thus finding fulfilment and happiness (the true end of education) in their own lives. There are of course exceptions to this. In every society there will be some saints, contemplatives, artists or even drop-outs, who reject not some part of the society, but its whole system of values and social organisation. A good society will have a high tolerance of such people and will benefit from them, but a form of education which regards this sort of reaction as the norm or the most admirable

33

will be destructive of the society and disastrous for the individual.

It is for a sixth form education conceived with these objectives and freed from the myths of the past that the next chapter outlines a programme in terms of content, teaching method and, in view of our heritage, examinations.

3

From objectives to content

The sixth form curriculum today

In discussing what and how sixth formers should learn and be taught in order to achieve the objectives set out in the previous chapter, it would be reasonable to start from what is happening now.

Nobody *knows*, of course, what has happened in the years since 1967, but at least we know what has not happened and it is possible to make some deductions about what has. Between 1967 and 1970 the total number of pupils in schools aged seventeen rose by 13·7 per cent, while the total number taking 'A' level courses rose only by 11·8 per cent. This is an indication that the pattern of sixth form education is becoming more diverse, but the difference is not great enough to suggest that the dominance of 'A' level has been seriously affected.

The essential thing which has not happened is that in spite of all the proposals and counterproposals outlined in the final chapter of this book, there has been no change in the sixth form examination system. Indeed, there has been no change in this system since GCE replaced the Higher School Certificate following the 1947 Report of the SSEC. Sixth form teachers often complain that they are 'fed up with continual changes' and plead to be 'left alone for a year or two to get on with the job'. 'Comprehensivisation' and the raising of the school leaving age have, of course, been great changes, but in the sixth form curriculum and examinations there have been no changes, only talk about changes. 'A' level has reigned unchanged, if not unchallenged, for a generation.

The main advantage claimed for having no prescribed sixth form curriculum but only external examinations is, like that for having no written constitution, flexibility; each student can make up for himself the pattern of examination subjects which best suits his own interests and career intentions; subjects which are hated can be dropped. There is truth in this claim. My own son, as a prelude to reading architecture at the university, took 'A' levels in history, zoology and mathematics. I doubt if any Continental system would have allowed for this combination.

In practice, however, there are great constraints on this freedom and flexibility. History, zoology and mathematics required a long struggle with the school authorities, which a parent who was not in the educational profession could not so easily have won. Most pupils find themselves in practice confined to the strictly limited patterns which the school provides in its normal timetable, a range of options no wider than the six tracks of the prescribed French baccalauréat and certainly less wide than the 'bizarre variations' (to use Crowther's term) open to and chosen by the American high school student. Moreover, the peculiarity of our own sixth form examination system, that, in spite of all attempts to reintroduce something like the old Higher School Certificate subsidiary subjects in the form of 'minors', 'electives', 'ancillaries', or 'qualifying levels', it still concentrates on so few subjects and those at 'A' level or nothing, means that the bias involved in choice of subject is more intense than in any other country.

The disadvantages are twofold. In the total pattern of the curriculum, it means there is no educationally determined plan and there are severe restrictions on the pupil's choice. The structure of 'A' levels or nothing for examined work leaves the conflicting forces of university faculty requirements, pupils' preferences and school organisation to fight it out as in a free but highly restricted market. Since it has been the university faculty requirements which controlled the most important rewards, it was almost inevitable that they should have proved the dominant influence and that general education, which enjoys theoretical approval, but brings no reward, should have been squeezed out. It is true that an unpublished survey carried out by Mr J. Selkirk at the University of Newcastle upon Tyne in 1970 and 1971 showed only 22 per cent of pupils responding that one of the 'A' levels they had chosen was 'made necessary by external requirements such as University entrance or some particular career demand', but one must make some allowance here, both for conditioning by the system and for the reluctance of sixth formers to admit that they are not acting as free agents. It is probably true that, given a choice between a three subject arts or science 'side', most sixth formers do consider that they have freely made the right choice; but this tells nothing of the choice they might have made in a different situation, where more subjects and at different levels were available.

The dominance of examinations

The second disadvantage is that, if the examinations are left dominant without any countervailing force from prescribed curriculum or syllabuses, the 'backwash' effect of examining methods on teaching methods is greatly increased. Few but those directly concerned realise to what extent the last two terms of the sixth form course are now dominated by revising for 'mock' 'A' levels, taking 'mock' 'A' levels, going over 'mock' 'A' levels and then almost immediately, beginning the process of re-revising for the real 'A' levels. It is hardly an exaggeration to say that for one-third of the two year course most pupils are engaged either in practising the technique of examination passing or in taking examinations. Many of the teachers themselves have become so affected by this system that they too have come to see the whole object of the course as passing the examinations, and strongly opposed a suggestion that these should be held earlier in the summer, on the grounds that once the examinations were over it would be impossible to retain the interest of their pupils, *because they would have nothing left to work for*. When, at the time of the national coal strike in 1972, a teacher was asked on a television programme whether the teachers could use similar tactics to secure their pay claim, he replied that they could not because the only section of the public which really suffered from a teachers' strike was 'children taking examinations'. Education unrelated to examinations could apparently be suspended without anybody minding very much.

Teachers have also come to love the examination system because it improves their relations with their pupils by putting them 'on the same side', in an alliance against the examiners. This is a very natural reaction and anything which brings teachers and pupils more closely into co-operation must be to that extent good; but joint shop-lifting campaigns and a common effort to outwit the police would have the same effect and could hardly be justified on those grounds alone. We need to examine, therefore, what kind of teaching and learning this co-operative effort to outwit the examiners involves. Fortunately this has been done for us very recently and authoritatively in D. P. M. Michael's *Guide to the Sixth Form*. Part of the significance of this book is that the author was President of the Association of Headmasters at the time of writing and the realism of his advice to sixth formers presumably represents the views of his colleagues and the actualities of the situation rather better than the somewhat high flown idealism of the Crowther

Report, or even of the *Sixth Form of the Future*. All quotations come from chapter 9:

> Especially when examination time draws near, a pre-conceived framework of study will help to preserve one from the temptation of spending too much time on work that has been found most attractive and that is for that very reason likely to be sufficiently well known.
>
> Inevitably in the conventional type of examination, a good memory is a tremendous asset, but the memory can be trained and improved ... Some may even find it an advantage to read aloud notes being revised; some may find it easier to imprint those same notes on the mind's eye. The mere copying and recopying of notes prompts the visual memory and the process of clarification and simplification fixes a subject in the mind ... Mnemonics are useful only as mechanical links between necessary facts ... A similar but less well known device, may be of some little help to the student. This consists of having prepared a whole series of images readily associated with numbers (for example, 1 one's self, 2 one's parents, 3 a triangle, 4 a dog, 5 a hand etc.).
>
> As the time of the examination approaches revision should become more and more intense.

When it comes to the actual day of the examination the advice is equally practical:

> The examinee should never begin to write immediately he sees the paper. There is first a plan of campaign to be settled. Consider the time available. Half a dozen questions in three hours should not be taken to permit a full half-hour for each question.

In fact, he recommends twenty-seven minutes for each question, allowing time for the plan of campaign and for revision.

> The order in which questions are tackled is important. As in window dressing, the best goods ought to be put first to catch the eye. More subtly, some effort should be made, provided that time is on the side of the candidate, to leave a good impression in the mind of the

examiner by delaying to the end a question which the candidate is confident of answering competently.

All this advice on how to study for 'A' level and how to get good results is, no doubt, very practical and the picture it presents of what the present curriculum really means to the pupil 'swotting for his "A" Levels' should be taken in conjunction with the Social Survey's revelation of the truth about 'general studies'. If we are to consider seriously changes that may alter the pattern of sixth form studies, we must see them against the realities of the situation for the average sixth former today, not against Crowther's 'deep emotional impulse to master one area of knowledge', even if this may be applicable to a small minority. As we have seen, the 'intensive revision' to which Mr Michael refers, is not just revision in May, at the last moment before the examination. For most sixth formers, revision, that is the memorisation of predigested facts, theories and opinions, begins half way through the second year of the course. By the time the day of the examination arrives, he has revised, practised and revised again until he is well prepared for the race against time and the battle with the examiners which Mr Michael describes.

It has often been pointed out that this sort of examination-oriented learning makes the transition from sixth form to university work particularly difficult. The Hale Report on teaching methods in universities points out (para. 64) that

even at the best, students coming to a university straight from school find themselves suddenly saddled with more responsibility for ordering their lives than they have had to take before; and in their approach to their subjects, many, perhaps most students on entry to university have hardly got beyond the stage of taking their opinions from authority and expecting to find the 'right' answers to all questions in a text book.

If this is a problem for those moving from sixth form learning to the comparatively similar activity of university learning, how much more acute it must be for those moving into active life. In a world where, for most people, work and leisure are still as strongly differentiated as they were for Aristotle, the prevailing experience of the creative 'play' activities of the sixth form is too 'scholarly' in its approach to lead on easily to the enjoyment of leisure, while the prevailing experience in the work-oriented disciplines is both too scholarly, too theoretical and too authoritarian to lead on easily to their application in practical life. The average sixth former finds that in the outside world there are no 'right answers' which can be 'revised', that if there were they would not be found in text books, that in most cases dealing with people is more important than dealing with ideas and that a sensible application of the simplest skills and concepts that he has absorbed in his sixth form mathematics, languages, social or physical sciences, rather than recall and operation of the most sophisticated, is what is really required of him.

An alternative curriculum

If it is agreed, then, that a curriculum of this kind, taught in this way, is inadequate to achieve the objectives outlined in the last chapter, we have alternative approaches to consideration of its improvement. We may assume that the tradition of an examination-oriented curriculum is too strong to be broken and approach it by trying to reform the examination system; or we may subject the curriculum and teaching methods themselves to a more fundamental criticism and then try to devise an examination system which would respond to the needs of the new curriculum. The first path may seem the more realistic and most proposals for reform since the Crowther Report have followed it, but in the space of fifteen years, they have achieved nothing, and it may, therefore, be worth attempting the second.

How then are we to translate the development of the

powers of the mind, in understanding and operation, the skills of communication and the capacity for enjoyment into school experiences, such as the teaching and learning of subjects?

Perhaps it is easiest to begin with communication, where there is, throughout Europe at least, a very wide measure of agreement. Few would deny that, at least up to the age of seventeen, students should continue the study of their own language, of a foreign language and of mathematics. In this country most pupils drop at least one of these and often two.

A better command of English, purely as a means of communication, oral as well as written, would be of value to every student, but English studies should include literature and drama, thus contributing to self-knowledge, moral education and enjoyment.

The study of a foreign language has also functions other than communication, but it is for communication, and above all oral communication, that it is most important. To have learnt to speak one foreign language effectively at school is an inducement to learn others at later stages in the process of life-long education: not to have done so is a barrier. But the learning of a foreign language can also contribute to an understanding of language in itself and so to our interpretation of our environment. Since it must surely be associated with learning something of the life and civilisation of the people who speak it, it contributes to our understanding of what Huxley called 'men and their ways' and to diminishing our ethnocentricity.

The study of mathematics has come to be seen in recent years as something akin to the study of a language, the universal language in which we express, and through which we manipulate, the quantifiable aspects of our experience. An understanding of mathematics and competence in certain simple skills has become essential to disciplines as different as the physical and biological sciences, the social sciences and philosophy, and therefore to our whole interpretation of our environment and our capacity to operate within it. It has also an important traditional function of exemplifying best the nature of symbolic reasoning. Why then do we, alone of European nations, not regard it as an essential part of upper secondary education?

The reason may be one which affects all the three media of communication which have been considered. This is the tradition that all subjects which are studied effectively in the sixth form at all must be studied approximately at the same level and to a prescribed examination syllabus which at least attempts to guarantee that level. Particularly in mathematics, it has been 'A' level mathematics or nothing, and it is not surprising that, given the choice, many have preferred nothing.

We need a sixth form curriculum in which everybody does English, but some more than others, everybody learns to speak and read a foreign language, but only the particularly gifted and interested study its literature (and then only for pleasure) and everybody gets an understanding of those mathematical concepts which underlie so much of the rest of our thinking, but only the gifted and interested go further.

It should be assumed also that these three media, which are media of education as well as of communication, will be taught operationally as well as academically.

By this I mean two things: the first is that much of the understanding which the pupil develops should be of that only half conscious type, based on experience, which we think of more as a skill, 'knowing how' and not 'knowing that': the second is that this is achieved by using what is learnt in concrete situations.

To learn to operate is not by any means the same thing as to learn to understand, although we often do understand better as a result of operating. We constantly carry out operations, such as riding a bicycle, without the least theoretic understanding of what we are doing. As

Polanyi has shown in *Personal Knowledge* (chapter 4) the actual physics of bicycling, 'the principle by which the cyclist keeps his balance', is quite unknown to the vast majority even of scientists. There are many things which we learn by example and practice: as Aristotle said, men learn to play the flute, without either the teacher or the learner understanding intellectually exactly why the thing is done in the way that it is.

This kind of personal and uncriticised knowledge may lie behind the morality of the 'virtuous peasant' who, like the Auvergnat farmer in *Le Chagrin et la pitié*, reacts with a fine and consistent moral judgment without ever having read a line of moral philosophy or being able to explain why he judges and acts as he does. It is in most areas of life at least as important as theoretical understanding and because it is more personal, *my* operational knowledge rather than universal intellectual knowledge, much more real and more stimulating to all except those who are temperamentally scholars. Unfortunately since examinations tend to be set and marked by those who are temperamentally scholars, it has been sadly neglected in the education of the sixth former.

To teach these subjects more operationally would not be difficult. English enters into most studies and many activities of life, and sixth form English should surely include creation as well as criticism, even if this is more difficult to examine. The student who is learning to *speak* German is, in the first sense used above, engaged in an activity which is more 'operational' than one who is studying the structure of the language and translating the written word. Moreover, he should, in the other sense of operational, be encouraged to use his growing knowledge of German both to read texts relevant to his other studies and for travel. Mathematics, at this basic level, should be taught as far as possible in such a way that it is used to solve problems and express relationships in other fields.

If these are essential areas of experience which most people would agree respond both to their objectives and to ours—assuming, that is, that a more operational and less daunting approach to mathematics can be found—how can we best reconcile the differing objectives and produce a balanced education over the rest of the curriculum? The answer surely lies in some prescribed pattern of 'disciplines', 'fields' or 'domains' of experience, combined with freedom of choice in the subject matter through which understanding in those domains is to be developed. Thus it seems reasonable to expect that if a man is to be free to understand and operate within the contemporary environment, he must have some understanding of the logical status of the exact sciences, of how their hypotheses are framed, their evidence assembled and treated, their theories reinforced or falsified. How much understanding of detail or of current theories and explanations he will need will depend on his future interests and intentions. If his interests lie that way and he is hoping to follow a scientific career at a university, a sixth former will obviously want to specialise to a very considerable extent in the exact sciences at school, but he will be incomplete as a human being if his education has taught him nothing of how to interpret his own nature and that of his fellow men, has contributed nothing to his moral development and given him no time or stimulation to develop his aesthetic creativity or enjoyment. The same is, of course, true in reverse of the sixth former who has concentrated entirely on languages and an associated social study and for whom the scientific interpretation of the world can easily become an alien, frightening and therefore rejected mystery.

Clearly, what should be our objective in the 'cognitive domain' is some sort of combination of breadth and depth which ensures that none of the main ways of interpreting our experience is so wholly neglected that it leaves the man more than he need be at the mercy of uncritical prejudice or charlatans, but allows sufficient concentration in a chosen field to respond to the deep emotional impulse where it really exists and, in more practical terms, to prepare the pupil for his chosen next step in life.

The forms of knowledge

Exactly how many separate ways of interpreting our experience we should take into account is open to question. Professor Hirst has suggested seven: mathematics and formal logic (where tests of truth are purely deductive), physical sciences, human sciences and history (which involve intuitive knowledge of the minds of other persons, their feelings and intentions), aesthetic, religious, moral and philosophical. In each of these the nature of 'knowledge' and the tests of truth which are appropriate are different.

From the point of view of practical curriculum planning, few would want to be more specific than that. Nor, of course, should we seek to establish a one-to-one relationship between these modes of thinking and corresponding school subjects. We have seen that 'English' as a school subject is important as a medium of communication, but that it also contributes to our understanding of ourselves and others and, by increasing our capacity for empathy, our critical judgment of conduct, and our identification with admired models, to our moral development. Drama and role playing in a sixth form English course can help the adolescent to recognise and accept his own nature and that of others. Here, and in creative writing, there is an operational element which the exigencies of examinations and the assumption that all subjects are taught 'for their own sake' and with the objective of producing 'scholars' in those subjects has too often squeezed out of the sixth former's experience, in favour of literary criticism which is often no more than the memorised criticism of earlier critics.

Most other 'subjects' contribute in this way to a number of objectives and with a sufficiently flexible system it would be possible for students (or their sixth form teachers acting as counsellors) to build their individual programmes by constructing a 'grid', such as is used by the compilers of multiple choice tests, and selecting a pattern of subjects, taken to different levels, which meets both our objectives in terms of general education and theirs in terms of interest and future intentions.

The Diploma in Higher Education and the International Baccalaureate

Two models for such a flexible system are the form of the Diploma in Higher Education proposed in the James Report on the education and training of teachers and that of the International Baccalaureate. The International Baccalaureate course has been designed for the two final years of secondary education in international schools (Peterson, *The International Baccalaureate*). It requires the student to follow courses in six subjects, of which three must be taken to the higher level (five or six periods a week) and three to a subsidiary level (five or six periods for one year or three for two). In addition, the equivalent of one half day must be available for creative and aesthetic activity, and every student must follow a course in the theory of knowledge, designed to bind together the different 'subjects' by bringing out the epistemological nature of the disciplines they represent. A 'distribution requirement' ensures that the three media of communication, the mother tongue, a foreign language and mathematics are included, as must be at least one subject drawn from the 'study of man' (e.g. history, psychology, social anthropology, geography, economics, etc.) and one from the experimental sciences (e.g. physical science, chemistry, biology, etc.). The sixth subject allows either for specialisation (e.g. mathematics, physics and chemistry at higher level, with English, German and social anthropology at subsidiary) or for the introduction of a more substantial involvement in an aesthetic subject. This distribution requirement ensures that none of the ways of interpreting our experience will be wholly neglected, but permits the student great freedom, both in the choice of emphasis and in the choice of subject area through which this emphasis is to be achieved. He cannot, as in the present sixth form, entirely neglect literature, nor mathematics nor foreign languages nor human experience, but he can choose both the level and the content of his involvement.

The proposals for the Diploma in Higher Education presented in the James Report are not dissimilar. True, we have here 'special' and 'general' studies rather than 'higher' and 'subsidiary' level subjects and, as is natural at a more advanced stage of education, there are no rigid distribution requirements; but the reasoning behind the structure of the Diploma follows very much the same lines as inspired the International Baccalaureate, as may be seen from the following quotations:

> Reference has already been made to the merits both of study in depth and of a broadly based education. These elements must be combined and interrelated, as 'special' and 'general' studies, in the Diploma in Higher Education. Such a synthesis would serve the needs of teachers without in any way diminishing the value and attractiveness to other students of the course proposed. In special studies the aim will be to encourage the student to pursue his chosen subjects in some depth and to acquire some degree of mastery of them. In general studies the aim will rather be to stimulate individual thought and discussion, to enable the student to realise the kind of problems and experiences that exist in fields outside his own, to make good the deficiencies in his intellectual and cultural awareness and above all to tempt him to further efforts of self-education in directions which he had not previously considered. (James Report, 4.8.)

One of the tasks of general education is to make good some of the cultural deficiencies of those who propose to be teachers of others. The course must therefore aim at providing some essential background in the main areas of human thought and activity, i.e. the humanities (above all literature), mathematics and the sciences (including their applications in practical situations), the social sciences, and the arts. (James Report, 4.10.)

Indeed, the teaching of almost any subject, to intending teachers and other students alike, should be illuminated by some awareness of its relationship to other areas of knowledge and its reference to the social, political, economic, cultural and technological conditions of contemporary society. (James Report, 4.15.)

It is objectives such as these that the International Baccalaureate, with its higher and subsidiary level subjects, its unifying course in the Theory of Knowledge and its offer of creative and aesthetic activity for all, seeks to achieve in the more structured situation of a sixth form.

Flexible programmes of this sort could provide for the needs both of the small proportion of genuine 'scholars', of whom the picture provided in the Crowther Report is not a travesty, and of the much larger number who will be seeking an education more closely related to life outside school and to operation rather than intellectual satisfaction.

In the United Nations International School, in New York, for instance, which in scholarly ability range is more comprehensive than our sixth forms are likely to be for many years, the International Baccalaureate forms the core of the curriculum for the last two years for all pupils, with the intellectually able and committed taking the full Diploma Course, while others take two or three I.B. courses along with a selection of programmes, designed by the school, and less challenging in purely intellectual terms. The same will presumably be true of the James

DipHE. If it is to have wide acceptance as an academic qualification, then not all entrants to colleges of education will be able to take the full Diploma. In the examples given in Appendix Six of the Report it is assumed that 800 out of a college of 1200 will be doing so. But there is no reason why all students should not participate in some DipHE courses and there is surely everything to be said for this kind of open-ended situation, rather than a rigid division between 'diploma streams' and others.

Much, of course, will depend upon how the courses are taught and this cannot be separated from how they are examined. Ideally, most sixth formers would probably like to see them taught with the real objectives as the paramount and openly specified aim. The fact that so few people ever discuss with them *why* they are following their sixth form courses, except to pass an examination and get a university place, is one of the things sixth formers resent.

This would surely involve an increasing involvement of the student in choosing and following his own plans of study, an increasingly operational approach for all but the small band of genuinely pre-committed scholars, an increasing realisation of the relationship between school work and adult non-school interests and activities. In fact, the teaching of 'A' level subjects is based on a quite different philosophy. This is that the subject, the discipline in itself, if pursued in a scholarly manner even by those whose interests are not scholarly and who are not going to be scholars when their full-time education is completed, has a special educational value of its own. History is taught in such a way that sixth formers may become as nearly as possible historians, literature that they may become as nearly as possible literary critics, science scientists, geography geographers and so forth. Virtually none of them are in fact going to become historians, literary critics, scientists or geographers, but the assumption is that, by some process of transfer of training, initiation into these disciplines will, automatically and in itself, equip them better to understand and to manipulate the quite different activities of their subsequent life. At least one can only assume that this is the underlying philosophy since, if it is not, it is impossible to make sense of the sixth form. The result of this philosophy and of the examinations which are based upon it is a teaching method the very reverse of that which we have suggested earlier. Instead of encouraging more and more individual study, using the library and resource centre, we have more and more taught periods. The average for an 'A' level subject, which in 1959 was seven, now seems to be eight or nine. It is perhaps significant that the James Report complains that this over-teaching extends into colleges of education (James Report, para. 4.16) since the majority of subject specialists in colleges of education have had their first experience as sixth form teachers. It is natural enough, as long as the teacher's function is largely seen as coaching the student to outwit the examiners in an 'A' level type of examination. But if students who leave sixth forms are to continue their education either at universities or in active life, surely they should be being introduced in the sixth form to the practice of self-education and to its media, libraries, television, correspondence courses and radio, much more than they at present are. They cannot expect in the next stage of their lives to be spoon-fed by a teacher and they are becoming increasingly unwilling to accept this at the sixth form level.

Again, if they are to learn to operate and to enjoy as well as to interpret and understand, they should surely be given more chance to do things, to create and get outside the walls of the school, than they are at present. It is true that the countries of Eastern Europe, and perhaps Maoist China, have found great difficulty in actualising the concept of polytechnical education and involving the sixth former in the work of farm and factory; but the intention is surely right. In our own society the growth of community service as a school activity has been rapid in the last few years, but it is a sad commentary on our sense of values that it has tended to be reserved for those who are not in the first flight in the more important activity of examination passing.

For it is the difficulty of assessing accurately in an examination this kind of operational involvement that has done most to deprive the sixth formers of it. Let me give two examples from the International Baccalaureate. In many subjects both we as examiners and they as students feel that the most educative part of their course is the individual study, which the student has pursued himself and which results in a four or five thousand word essay, based, in sixth form terms, on personal research. Yet it is constantly asked how much weight an examiner should give to this when there is so little certainty in checking that it is the candidate's own work? Again, in the proposed course on the Culture of Cities, an important element should be the student's own practical involvement in social work in his own city and the operational understanding that he gains from that. Yet how is this to be fairly and impartially assessed in an examination system, when the difference between a grade B and a grade C on a five-point scale may mean acceptance to or rejection from the privileged group of university students?

Teaching methods are inevitably determined by examination methods, and as long as there are more young people seeking entry to the next stage of education than that stage can accept, examiners are going to be pressured, as they are now, into giving the most weight to those performances which can be most accurately, most reliably and most defensibly assessed. Yet these may not be, indeed often are not, the performances resulting from the kind of teaching and learning which is in reality most valuable to the sixth former. This is the dilemma. Is there any way out?

4

Teaching methods and organisation

Teaching methods in the new sixth form

If it is agreed that the objectives of sixth form education can best be achieved in the foreseeable future through such a flexible and balanced range of 'subjects', three questions remain for discussion in this chapter. How should they be taught? Within what age range should they be taught? and where should they be taught?

As far as the methods of sixth form teaching are concerned, we surely need, as the James Report suggests for the DipHE, to seek ways of combining breadth and depth; but we have also got to seek ways of combining operational with intellectual learning. Nor must we expect the ideal mixture to be the same for every pupil. Nothing is likely to lose the goodwill of the expanding numbers of sixth formers, with their very different approaches to learning, than a system which imposes the same programme on every one or which values, almost to the exclusion of all other types of learning, either the reality or the imitation of 'scholarship' which is appropriate as an objective only to the tiny minority of 'scholars'. 'Breadth' and 'depth' are two of the most over-used and under-classified concepts in the literature of education.

Let us at least try to illustrate in reasonably concrete terms what we mean by combining them.

One quite frequent but rather naïve interpretation of the tension between breadth and depth is purely in terms of information. 'Breadth' in this sense means having a lot of factual knowledge and perhaps some inert ideas about a wide variety of fields or a wide range within a single field; 'depth' having an equal amount of factual knowledge or inert ideas about a very narrow field.

Thus a sixth former who knows the date and principal standardised 'causes' of not only the French, but the English, Russian, Mexican and Chinese revolutions is considered to have had a broad historical education, while one who knows only the French revolution but can identify also the minor characters and knows not only the years but the months in which certain events took place and has learnt the 'accepted' interpretations of their significance, is considered to have had a deep one. Or a pupil who has factual recall of an outline course in six subjects has had a broad education, and one who has factual recall of one intensive course in a narrow field, a deep one. Or a pupil who can express himself fluently, but inaccurately in three languages is broadly educated and one who knows only Latin, but in that never makes a grammatical mistake, is deeply educated.

All this seems something of a travesty of the issue. Broad education does *not* mean knowing the date of the Treaty of Utrecht as well as the formula for sodium chloride and deep education does not mean knowing all the Latin nouns ending in -io which are masculine.

If this is what the distinction does not mean, it is admittedly rather more difficult to establish what it does. Perhaps it will help to remind ourselves of the purpose of sixth form education. It is, surely, not to produce memory banks of either general or specialised information; it is to produce people who, while retaining all their other human potentialities, have been taught to think and, having thought, to make wise decisions.

In the ordinary course of our lives we do need to think both broadly and deeply and we do need to make decisions. We need to be able to relate, to connect our thinking about a specific problem to a wide range of interests and we also need to think accurately in detail, 'deeply' if you like, about a particular element in it. If, for instance, an industrialist is planning to locate a factory, he ought to consider purely geographical factors, such as transport and proximity to markets and raw materials, social factors such as the availability of a labour force, socio-moral factors such as the availability of decent housing for his workers, aesthetic factors such as the effect of his factory on the environment, and many others. He cannot be expected to be an expert in all these areas, but if he is an educated man and a member of a civilised society, his education should have been sufficiently broad to make him at least aware of the many dimensions affecting his choice and capable of judging and balancing the expert opinions about them that are put before him.

At the same time, however, there are fields in which he, and he alone, is the authority, in which he can say that whatever others may say about housing or amenity or transport, this or that location simply will not do for the specialised production on which he is an expert.

This is perhaps a naïve illustration, but it is at least an attempt to explain why both breadth and depth of learning is relevant to the real needs of real people who have to decide real issues in the contemporary world. It could be repeated for school teachers, town clerks, army officers or indeed all forms of employment which sixth formers enter either with or without a subsequent university education. It is also, I believe, true of the best of scholars, and those who have not got it become not the best of scholars, but Browning's 'Grammarian'. Is it not true also of our personal lives, our enjoyment of our world and our communication with our fellow men?

The difference between education in breadth and depth here is surely that in the broad context the educated individual is aware of the factors and the values involved over the whole range of relevant experience, has thought about them enough to realise their importance and in very general terms to be critical, but normally accepts, without personally working them out, the received opinions of experts. This may seem to some of today's extreme libertarians a shockingly conformist attitude; but in fact what else can we do? We cannot be sufficiently expert in every field each to form our own conclusions and, as it were, to re-create the whole of human knowledge or the whole value system of the human race in the experience of each individual. On the other hand if we have *no* experience in one of these major fields, we may be tempted to assume that it, the moral, perhaps, the aesthetic or the technological, does not matter at all, or else, if we think it does matter, to be unable to understand what the experts in it are saying. Education in depth, on the other hand, means that in a limited area the individual has at least begun to understand, from his own experience, how the received opinions are formulated and what processes of intellectual rigour and accuracy are needed to arrive at them or to question them.

How, then, are we to give pupils at the sixth form level an experience of what it means to think deeply and accurately, while at the same time developing the full range of their capacity to interpret, act upon and enjoy their environment? One answer, at least, is that the combination, mediated as in practice it must be through school subjects, should operate at two levels. In the total pattern of subjects studied some can be deeper areas of concentration than others. Thus an International Baccalaureate student taking higher level mathematics, physics and chemistry, but subsidiary level English, German and social anthropology, could be held, in one sense, to be studying natural science in 'depth', but arts and social studies in 'breadth'. But this is a very imprecise formulation. Even a university honours degree course, if for instance it attempts to cover the whole of English literature in three years, may be less deep and more broad than an 'A' level course, which concentrates over two years on five or six set books. We must, therefore, consider the second level, not merely the distribution of subjects but the syllabus, the pattern of study, within each subject.

Here the German concept of 'learning from examples', or, as we would say in this country, 'topics' or 'special subjects' may provide the answer. A modern history or physics course which combines a broad outline of the field as a whole with very detailed study of a special topic, demanding accuracy, judgment and the rigorous evaluation of evidence, is giving the pupil, within the area of a single subject, experience of both 'breadth' and 'depth'. If it is well taught, the relationship between them can be brought out by the teacher, so that a sixth form curriculum which brings together a well calculated distribution of subjects, studied in this way, teaches not only what it means to study in depth and in breadth, but also their relationship. If, as in the International Baccalaureate, a deliberate attempt is made to ensure that the pupil is conscious of the differing methodologies of the subjects and of the difference between broad generalisations and deeply specialised investigation, then he should be well prepared both for university work and for practical life.

There remains the problem of combining intellectual and operational experience of the subjects, using the word 'subject' in its widest sense to indicate areas of experience. Something has already been said in chapter 3 of ways in which a more operational approach to the traditional subjects could be achieved. It may be, however, that if we are ready to make a reality of the operational approach, we shall have to introduce into the sixth form curriculum new subjects, more closely related to the intellectual interests and activities of life outside the school.

It is difficult to see, for instance, why if history, geography, chemistry and even engineering science are educative experiences at sixth form level, accountancy, architecture and social anthropology should not be. After all, engineering science is essentially the application of mathematics to the design and control of machinery and accountancy the application of mathematics to the design and control of business operations. What is surely needed is the inclusion of those intellectual disciplines which contribute to operation in the world which the majority of the pupils are actually going to enter and not solely to those which were studied in universities seventy years ago and have therefore established themselves as 'school subjects'. The main practical objection to such an expansion of the range of sixth form subjects is, of course, that we have few or no teachers capable of teaching them. We may find that this has some bearing both on the third topic of this chapter and on the practical possibilities of development discussed in the next. Before proceeding to them, however, we should be clear about what age range of pupils we are expecting to cater for.

The age range of the new sixth form

It was hinted in chapter 1 that a title such as 'fifteen to eighteen' would not have done for this book because the age range of the sixth form was one of the things which was bound to come in question.

In fact, although there is a very clear trend in Europe and America to treat sixth form, or upper-secondary, education as a separate phase in the whole educational process, there is much less agreement about the age range it should cover. The average German or Swedish student leaving the upper class of the *Gymnasium* and entering the university is already nearly twenty-one, an age at which the youngest of his English contemporaries may have taken their first degrees. At the other end of the scale, it is still reasonably frequent for pupils in Scotland or North America to enter college or university before their eighteenth birthday.

It is worth considering, therefore, in relation to our own future, at what stage in the average young person's life this combination of general education in breadth with the first experience of specialised education in depth, whether intellectual or operational, should take place.

The European example is not necessarily one to follow. The high age range of the sixth form in many European countries is due to the practice of 'repeating' which, fortunately, is much rarer with us. Repeating means quite simply that if a pupil, at any stage in his education, but quite often in the final upper-secondary stage, fails to satisfy the authorities that he has adequately covered the course, in all its branches, he is compelled to 'stay down' and repeat the entire year. Only too often this means going over again exactly the same ground in all his subjects, many of which he satisfactorily completed, with the same teachers, in the same way, but now as a member of a group of pupils most of whom are a year younger than himself and doing the course for the first time. The practice is vehemently criticised in all the countries where it prevails. It is, indeed, difficult to conceive anything more likely to render impossible the achievement of one of our major objectives—the stimulation of a continued desire to learn and to benefit from life-long education.

To assume that we should move in the other direction and make the transfer from secondary to tertiary education at seventeen, merging the last year of the sixth form and the first year of higher education in a DipHE type of course for all, is more attractive, but it might be considered too radical a change. The truth is surely that young people mature, both intellectually and personally at very different rates. Both forms of maturity are important and it seems to me as unwise to admit to higher education

intellectual prodigies of sixteen as to exclude late deve-
lopers of twenty. Would it not be best if at least as a
first stage each individual student started on a sixth form
course of the type described above at the moment when
he is 'ready' for it, a concept not unknown to primary
school teachers in relation to such skills as reading.

The location of the new sixth form

The question then remains where this course should be
given. The range of alternatives at present possible in
England and Wales is surprisingly wide. The sixth form at
present may be:

(a) The last two or three years of an academically
    selective 11–18 grammar school
(b) The last two or three years of a 13–18 school, often
    independent and selective by wealth, but less selec-
    tive by attainment.
(c) The last two or three years of a non-selective 11–18
    comprehensive school.
(d) Two or three years in a separate, academically selec-
    tive institution, a 'sixth form college'.
(e) Two or three years in a separate non-selective insti-
    tution, a 'junior college'.
(f) Two or three years in a college of further education.
(g) Two or three years in a college combining further
    education and upper-secondary education.

No one can say that we have not in this country allowed
freedom of experiment in arranging the institutional
setting of the sixth form.

The benefit to be derived from all this experiment is
surely that we ought to be able, gradually, to determine
which pattern will provide the best available education,
within the limits of the present and foreseeable restraints,
for all our sixth formers. It may be that we have not
yet gained enough experience from our diversity and that

it would be premature to plump for one solution rather than the others, but it does seem probable that we have reached a stage where certain solutions ought to be ruled out, and where we should be beginning to put more and more of our resources into those which seem, if not definitely, at least probably, preferable. In doing so, it is going to be very important to remember that what we are asking ourselves is not whether any of the patterns listed above is good in a particular school, given the necessary resources; but which of the patterns is best for the schools of the country as a whole, given a reasonably even division of the resources between them. The whole controversy over comprehensive education has been vitiated by concentration on the question of whether it lowers the standards of education for the 20 per cent of pupils from former grammar schools, without adequately considering whether it raises them for the 80 per cent from former secondary moderns.

The form which can most safely be ruled out is, strangely enough, the classic model on which traditional thinking about the sixth form is based: the selective top of a selective eleven-to-eighteen grammar school.

When we are able to look at the development of English school systems in a sufficiently long historical perspective, we shall surely see that this type was a historical accident which happened to meet very well the needs of a rapidly changing society in a relatively short transitional period. When, after 1902 and under the influence of Morant, the grammar schools were developed to give all middle-class children and bright working-class children a 'maintained' equivalent to the upper-class public school, no one intended those schools to have an eight-year age range. The public schools had a four- to five-year age range from thirteen, and the grammar schools were expected to have a four- to five-year age range from eleven. But the grammar schools 'grew tops' and these tops were the nostalgically regretted pre-war sixth forms—average numbers

61

twenty. They were, as I have suggested earlier, good places in their day for teaching and learning, and in the much more hierarchical society of the inter-war years, they had a social role in the school. But they could not survive the post-war advent of mass secondary education, accelerated 'staying-on' and the change in social attitudes.

Even if the selective eleven-to-eighteen grammar school were not on its way out all over Europe, the long age range would be proving, as it is in those grammar schools which remain, unmanageable in conditions where staying on into the sixth form is the rule rather than the excep-tion. Thus we see in more and more of our remaining grammar schools, as in comprehensives, the creation of a 'sixth form block' and the treatment of the sixth form as a separate entity within the school, rather than an inte-grated 'top' to a unified society.

But the grammar school, selecting at eleven, is fading into the past in any case. What is perhaps even more surprising is that the next candidate for elimination is the top of the much favoured 'eleven-to-eighteen purpose-built comprehensive'. The case against this type of sixth form needs much more careful analysis. It is indeed the crucial issue before us.

Circular 10/65, supported, it seems, at the time by the majority of those who favoured comprehensive reorgani-sation, allowed for the possibility of a number of alter-native patterns, but clearly pointed to the eleven-to-eigh-teen, all-through, purpose-built comprehensive as the ideal towards which, in the long run, we should strive. I pro-pose to argue that not only is this ideal fundamentally misconceived, but that if we were able to achieve it on a national scale it would destroy the sixth form.

The eleven-to-eighteen grammar school may have been a historical accident, but the eleven-to-eighteen compre-hensive, inheriting the accidental age range, is also a geographical anomaly. When a country finds itself with an institutional pattern which is *both* a historical accident *and* a geographical anomaly, there is a good prima facie case for suspecting that something may have gone wrong. This is the case with our eight-year comprehensives. It is true that the USSR and USA have long had comprehensive secondary education and that by now most European countries are adopting it; but nowhere, save in England and Wales, is it being provided in a single institution with an age range from eleven to eighteen. Either one finds a shorter period of unitary secondary education, e.g. from twelve to seventeen, or, as in Scandinavia, France and Italy the upper-secondary stage, the nearest equivalent to our sixth form, is provided in a separate institution, the new *Lycée* or *Gymnasium*.

The reasons for making a break at some point between eleven plus and eighteen plus have been rehearsed often enough to need no more than restatement here in summary form. The all-through comprehensive must necessarily be very big, if it is to produce a viable sixth form, and we are becoming increasingly concerned with the impersonality of large institutions. It is true, of course, that decentralisation through tutor groups or house systems can mitigate the impersonality of the large school for the pupil, but these are not always as meaningful to the pupil as their designers hope. More dangerous to the maintenance of good human relations may be the very large, and often very transient staff of teachers in a big all-through school. The point made long ago by Professor Pedley, that we could not physically aim for a general pattern of large all-through schools without scrapping, at enormous expense, a great part of our existing secondary provision, should not, perhaps, be used as a theoretical criticism, but it does surely mean that the onus of proof lies on the advocates of the more expensive pattern. More important is the social argument that so wide an age range presents particular problems in the relations between staff and pupils. Attitudes and controls which are acceptable between teachers and school children of eleven or twelve are no longer acceptable between tutors and sixth formers. There must be a transition from one pattern to the other in the course of full-time education, but within a single institution the transition can be quite difficult to make. It is this more than anything else which is leading to the rapid development of sixth form blocks and centres.

The size of the new sixth form

The final argument is a statistical one and particularly relevant to the sixth form. It arises from trying to answer the question: how large does a sixth form need to be if it is to cater adequately for the needs and interests of all its members? To try to answer it involves entering the very problematical areas of manpower planning and the prediction of people's behaviour.

There have been a number of estimates of the 'viable' size of a sixth form and they have tended to rise as the years went on. In 1967-8, for instance, the average size of grammar school sixth forms had risen to just over a hundred and that of comprehensives to just under fifty. A much quoted figure in the following year was 120 (*The Times Educational Supplement*, 3.10.69) and the HMA document *The Sixth Form of the Future* (September 1968) noted (p. 65, in italics): 'Indeed the greatest danger inherent in many current schemes for re-organisation lies in a proliferation of inadequate sixth forms in response to circular 10/65', and considered that an all-through school would require a twelve form entry (i.e. an enrolment of well over 2,000) to produce a sixth form of viable size.

Viability has generally been held to depend on two factors, the capacity to offer pupils a reasonable choice of subjects, more than one foreign language, for instance, or economics as well as history and geography, and the provision of more than one specialist teacher in each subject. The latter proviso is important not merely because if all sixth form history teaching is in the hands of one history teacher the pupils may get rather a one-sided view, but because unless history can be timetabled in parallel sets and in more than one slot in the week, the combinations of subject which pupils may choose are severely limited. If a sixth form is to be viable, it must be able to satisfy these criteria without producing teaching groups in any subject which remain consistently and unreasonably small. What is 'unreasonable' is a matter of judgment, but sixth formers do teach and criticise each other, and my own estimate would be that to belong to a group of less than eight was a positive disadvantage to the pupil, and that to ask a highly qualified teacher to teach a group of less than twelve was to make less than the best use of scarce resources.

The ILEA survey in 1968 (*Sixth Form Opportunities in Inner London*) suggested that a sixth form offering twelve subjects (e.g. English, mathematics; history, geography, economics; Latin, German, French; physics, chemistry, biology and art) would need to have between eighty and ninety pupils, if no teaching group was to fall below five. It is easy to see, therefore, why the minimum viable size even for a traditional sixth form must now be regarded as something nearer two hundred. But will the traditional sixth form meet our current needs? The range of subjects quoted above is excessively meagre, even for an 'academic' sixth form, leaving no opportunity either for experiment or for such minority interests as music, Spanish, Russian, engineering science or geology. The introduction of new, more operational courses, of the kind proposed above would be impossible, and no provision is made for the 'new sixth former' following other than 'A' level courses. Compared with the thirty 'A' level subjects and wide range of 'O' level, CSE and vocational courses offered at Southampton College for Girls, or thirty-seven 'A' level courses at Luton Sixth Form College, it seems like a reversion to the pre-war grammar school sixth.

The more cogent become the arguments for expanding

the size of the sixth form, and therefore of the sixth form teaching staff, the clearer it becomes that to insist on a general pattern of all-through comprehensives each with its own sixth form top, would be to sacrifice the sixth form to the demands either of politicians who have become mystically attached to 'the Bill, the whole Bill and nothing but the Bill', as a measure of social engineering, or to those of teachers who cannot bear to see *their* school without its sixth form.

How, for instance, would such sixth forms be staffed? Mumford calculated in 1970 (*Comprehensive Reorganisation and the Junior Colleges*, p. 6) that if the whole of secondary education were provided through a network of all-through comprehensives of 1,500 pupils, then each school could expect on its staff one good honours graduate in mathematics, 0.8 of a chemist and 0.6 of a physicist. Such calculations are very fallible of course, as is all manpower forecasting. The slump in graduate employment may once more be diverting an additional supply of scientists into the schools, some of whom may decide to remain there—though I would rate this as more probable if they found themselves in sixth form centres or colleges than in all-through comprehensives. What remains incontrovertible is that a pattern of all-through comprehensives would provide more and smaller sixth forms than any other. 'In sum,' writes L. C. Taylor (*Resources for Learning*, p. 56) 'for reasons we have examined, comprehensive reorganisation in its most popular "all-through" shape requires a new army of graduates to man a multiplicity of smaller sixth forms, or a vast rebuilding programme.' In my opinion it would need both.

Patterns of sixth form

If we rule out the possibility that every all-through secondary school should have its own sixth form, we are left with a choice between five patterns, the thirteen- or fourteen-to-eighteen upper school, the 'mushroom' sixth form growing out of one secondary school, as at Mexborough, and taking in pupils from a satellite group of eleven-to-sixteen schools, the selective 'academic' sixth form college, the unselective 'general' college, and the combination of sixth form and further education, in what might be called, in American terms, the community college. It would probably be wise to continue a bit longer with experiments of all these types, though my own feeling is that the development of sixth form centres in public schools shows that the natural break comes at the beginning of the sixth form.

Of the various sixth form patterns, the 'mushroom' type has many of the marks of a transitional expedient. It has the practical advantage of building on an existing sixth form and the 'political' one that it allows what was previously the grammar school to retain its sixth form, being fed by a number of previously secondary modern schools. As a long term proposition, however, it has serious disadvantages. It can hardly be easy to avoid altogether the danger of tension between the home-grown and the immigrant sixth formers, and if there is any truth in the argument that a break at sixteen will discourage staying-on, this is most likely to happen when it involves transfer, not to an independent college, where all will start equal, but to another school. Moreover the 'mushroom', by retaining its stalk of eleven- to sixteen-year-olds retains one of the major social problems of the all-through comprehensive. It seems more likely, and more desirable, therefore, that this type of sixth form will die out having served its purpose, and the 'tadpole tails' drop away, as they have at Southampton.

As between the other three types, it may be premature to judge. The most important issue seems to be one which has, until very recently, been curiously neglected in discussions of the sixth form, the relationship between schools and colleges of further education.

67

A tidy pattern, for instance, and one which would be in line with what some other European countries have done would be to concentrate the academic, largely pre-university sixth formers in the sixth form colleges as has been done at Stoke, and provide for all the rest in the College of Further Education. This might be popular with existing sixth form teachers and the arguments against 'selection at sixteen' do not seem nearly so strong today as those against selection at 'eleven plus'.

It is hardly realised, however, what an upheaval such a scheme would involve. The justification of it would, presumably, be rationalisation, that is the avoidance of duplication in 'A' level teaching and the allocation to each type of institution of a clearly defined role in the education of the sixteen- to eighteen-year-olds. To achieve this it would have to involve the suppression of 'A' level classes in the colleges of further education, except, presumably, for adults. A few figures of what is happening now will show what a drastic interference with current patterns of growth that would mean. In 1969, the latest year for which comparable statistics are available, more than 10 per cent of all pupils taking 'A' level, within the school age range, were doing so in colleges of further education. This was in spite of considerable pressure to remain in school to take them, and the growth rate of 'A' levels in colleges has, over the last few years been faster than that in schools. In March 1972 the President of the Head Masters Association marked the end of the traditional opposition of the schools to the offer of 'A' level in the colleges. Students aged sixteen-to-nineteen should be free to choose, he said in his presidential address, whether they want to attend a school or a college of further education (*Guardian*, 20.3.72).

Another objection to the clear-cut demarcation is that it would render the provision of 'A' level courses in the colleges for the growing number of adults who now take them (nearly five thousand in 1969) much more difficult.

It may be, of course, that the drift of teenagers out of school and into the colleges of further education to take their 'A' levels has been caused by the social tensions of the all-through school, a dislike, for instance, of pre-fecthood, hockey and dress regulations. If this is true, it might well reverse itself when the choice was no longer between school and college, but between sixth form college and further education college. Perhaps for that reason, the sixth form college ought not to be ruled out, but it does not, in fact, seem to be proving very popular; and even some colleges like Luton, which started as academic sixth form colleges, are now becoming open entry junior colleges.

The open entry junior college, now established by at least ten LEAs and planned by many more, accepts into its sixth form all those who wish to remain at school after 'O' level, CSE or the age of sixteen. It can offer a very wide range of 'A' levels, as well as 'O' level, the new CEE or vocationally orientated courses, often combined with some sort of work experience. It has begun to provide evidence that the break at sixteen, if it means moving to a college of this type, does not discourage staying-on, as some people have feared. Southampton which started these colleges in 1966 has produced a table (Table 2) of the numbers of students who have transferred into the junior colleges, classified by the number of 'O' level/CSE Grade 1 passes which they had before entry.

The growth has been greatest among those with less qualifications, but one of the things which the colleges are also showing is that those with very minimal initial qualifications, who enter a junior college, may develop an undiscovered talent for academic work. The Director of Education for Southampton reports: 'From experience since 1967, the Heads of secondary colleges are convinced that a student's degree of motivation is of the greatest importance for future success and more so than any

Table 2.

Numbers of students transferred into junior colleges

Year	A	B	C	D
1967	75	52	38	19
1968	84	81	69	39
1969	86	75	103	83
1970	101	93	126	75*

A, 5 or more; B, 3 or more; C, 1 or 2; D, none.

* I am indebted for this table, as for much more in this chapter, to an unpublished thesis on the Sixth Form College by T. J. Foulkes (Oxford University Department of Educational Studies, 1971).

measure of intelligence or academic attainment at any previous stage of a child's development, whether 11+ or 16+' (D. P. J. Browning: 'The Development of Open Access Secondary Colleges in Southampton', July 1971, quoted in Foulkes, op. cit.). This is exactly the argument which my fellow headmasters of grammar schools were using in 1947 when they first began to find entry to their schools determined by selection tests which took no account of the child's motivation or the parent's backing.

But the very acceptance of the open access junior college, as potentially a better answer than the 'mushroom' or the academic college, raises immediately the question of its relations with the college of further education. If both establishments provide both 'A' levels and vocational courses, what is the difference between them? Why should not both provide courses leading to the ONC and OND? Why, in fact, should there be two types of establishment at all?

It is not surprising, therefore, that a number of authorities are beginning to experiment with a single college which combines what has been traditionally regarded as the sixth form with what has been traditionally regarded as 'further education'. For the moment these experiments are confined to the south-west but the advantages over maintaining two separate institutions, particularly in small towns with a large rural hinterland, are so obvious that the experiment seems likely to spread.

These advantages are not only administrative and economic. The college of further education has a tradition of more operational courses which could be of great value to the sixth form; the contact with day release pupils from industry could, in the opinion of some judges, be salutary for both day release students and sixth formers; the problem of who is to teach the newer, more operational courses might be more easily solved by bringing in people from active life, as part-time teachers, in a further education context; and the gradual introduction of teaching methods more appropriate to life-long education in an adult community might be easier in such a setting.

On the other hand, there are some suspicions that traditions of pastoral care on the part of teachers and attendance on the part of pupils are weaker in further education than in the sixth form, and a fear that the merging of the sixth form and the college of further education might lead to the loss of some of the most cherished values of sixth form education. The evidence of Table 57 in the Government Social Survey, para. 163, did not seem to bear out these fears, but this is probably the crucial issue on which a lot more evidence needs to be accumulated from the schemes now being initiated, before a decision can be reached.

It is our good fortune that the extreme decentralisation of educational planning in this country is going to give us the evidence, drawn from almost every type of sixth form organisation, from which we can gradually work out a nationally acceptable solution.

5

The process of change

The pattern before the Crowther Report

If our administrative system provides us with an unrivalled opportunity for trying out different systems of sixth form organisation, the reverse is true about the sixth form curriculum. The history of the quarter-century since the end of the Second World War is anything but encouraging to those who believe that changes in the content of sixth form education are needed. These must, presumably, include the majority of rational men, since the stream of proposals for change since the publication of the Crowther Report has been almost continuous. Moreover it would be very strange indeed if, in a generation which has seen such dramatic changes in the whole structure of our society, the content of upper-secondary education had been the one area where no changes of any sort were desirable. Yet, in fact, no changes of any significance have taken place. The purpose of this chapter is to examine the proposals for change which have been made and the reasons why none of them have been adopted. As a result of this examination it may be possible to suggest changes in our procedure for arriving at educational decisions which would make change possible in future, and to sketch the lines upon which, once the log jam is broken, a new pattern of sixth form education might be based.

The post-war era started with high hopes in education (or, some people would say, with starry eyes) just as it did in so many other areas of social life. The Butler Act was introducing secondary education for all and the Norwood Report had recommended the abolition of external examinations at fifteen or sixteen, the much criticised School Certificate. Recommendations (8) and (9) of the Report read:

> Up to the age of 18+ all pupils should either receive full-time education or be brought under the influence of part-time education, and full consideration should be given to the educational and social advantages of the performance of public service for a period of six months falling between school and University or other courses of higher education.
>
> In the interest of the individual child and of the increased freedom and responsibility of the teaching profession change in the School Certificate Examination should be in the direction of making the examination entirely internal, that is to say, conducted by the teachers at the school on syllabuses and papers framed by themselves.

In fact, neither of these things happened and the forces of conservatism, both within the teaching profession and the outside world, turned the new GCE into something barely distinguishable from the old School Certificate. The one difference was that since the GCE was a 'subject' examination, with no requirement to pass in a balanced range of subjects, as there had been in the School Certificate, the examination's influence on the balance of the curriculum passed from some kind of at least semi-public control to the arbitrary influence of university admission officers. If matriculation requirements ceased to demand English or a foreign language from science candidates, then all the forces of competition began to operate in favour of committed 'scientists' dropping these subjects as soon as possible.

The total failure of the recommendation that subjects should not be taken at 'O' level by those who were carrying them on to 'A' level should have acted as a warning to subsequent reformers. Yet the same mistake was made in this country by the proposers of 'Q' and 'F' and in France when, after the abolition of part one of the Baccalaureate (their equivalent of 'O' level), the BEPC was introduced, designedly only for those who did not intend to go on to the Baccalaureate, but now taken by almost everybody.

It can now be stated almost as an educational law that if a nationally administered external examination is available at this age it will be taken by all pupils at this age, whether it is intended for them or not. Such examinations are like mountains: people take them because they are there. The teachers like them because they motivate pupils to follow courses which might not otherwise engage their interests; the pupils like them because they provide some sort of objective, however spurious; and the parents like them because they cannot be *sure* that their children will reach their intended objective of the next public examination, and therefore regard them as an insurance—at least one piece of paper in the adolescent's pocket. Thus, future university physicists still take 'O' level physics and future polytechniciens, the BEPC.

At the university entrance level there was an additional change, the abolition of the 'subsidiary level' examinations. In retrospect, and considering the constant efforts that have been made since 1959 to reintroduce examined courses at a level somewhere between 'O' level and 'A' level, the abolition of the subsidiary subjects now seems strange. The reason given at the time was part of the general attempt to reduce the amount of external examinations. The normal pattern in schools had been to take the school certificate in the fifth year, four subsidiary

74

levels in the sixth and two higher and two repeated subsidiary levels in the seventh. A less drastic way of achieving the same end might have been for the Ministry of Education, as it then was, to forbid the taking of subsidiary levels except in association with higher levels at the end of the course.

This would have achieved the same object of freeing the first year sixth from external examinations, but it would have involved direct intervention by the Ministry in the control of curriculum. As long as the fiction was preserved that examinations were provided by autonomous university-based examining boards, and schools were free to use them or not as they pleased, the only way to ensure that subsidiary levels were not taken twice was to persuade Boards to abolish them altogether.

The new sixth form curriculum, controlled by the pressure of competition for university places, exercised through the GCE 'A' level, remained unchallenged until the publication of the Crowther Report in 1959.

The Crowther Report and first reactions

This report expressed concern about the premature and excessive degree of specialisation in the existing system, noting particularly the 'illiteracy' of the scientists and 'innumeracy' of the arts and humanity students which it was producing. As a remedy it proposed a common six period a week science course for all in the middle school and endorsed the mythical one-quarter-to-one-third of the sixth former's time given to general studies, recommending that some steps (it was never quite clear what) should be taken to ensure that this time was not 'neglected and wasted'. Neither recommendation was implemented. This is not surprising since no machinery existed for implementing them. In fact, as we have seen in chapter 3, the pressures of competition actually worsened the situation which Crowther criticised.

75

Since no official machinery which could influence the sixth form curriculum existed, the first two attempts to remedy the situation were the result of private initiatives. They are of interest mainly because their failure illustrates two types of approach which have been shown not to work.

Professor Boris Ford tried to secure Crowther's objectives by seeking the voluntary co-operation of the schools. A considerable number of schools pledged themselves to observe his 'Agreement to Broaden the Curriculum'. The terms of the A.B.C. were to keep open a genuine choice between arts and science until the end of the fifth year (Crowther had shown that most pupils were effectively forced to make this choice at the age of thirteen or fourteen) and to devote a genuine one-third of the sixth form timetable to non-specialist work. Some schools undoubtedly stuck to their bargain, but the pressures of competition were too much for most of them, as the evidence already quoted from the Social Survey abundantly shows. Those familiar with industrial negotiations will recognise the normal fate of declarations of intent—a brief and patchy period of influence, followed by collapse before the pressure of the market.

The second private initiative was my own. It was based on the theory that if there was no machinery for imposing a general reform, and if general reform by voluntary action was impracticable, there might be some chance for a small-scale pilot project which might demonstrate that some of the dangers feared from a broader curriculum were illusory. After the publication of the Gulbenkian Report, therefore, we held a number of conferences at Oxford and began to assemble a group of thirty schools who would be prepared to co-operate in adopting a sixth form programme of four 'A' levels (including both arts and science subjects) at seven periods a week each, plus seven periods of general studies. A pilot project of this kind would have required the agreement of the universities, perhaps even faculty by faculty, to accept a slightly lower standard from our 'four "A" level' candidates than was currently expected from the normal 'three "A" level' candidates. Moreover the schools, the pupils and the parents would have had to be prepared to take a certain risk. The pattern itself was not by any means ideal, but was forced on us by the necessity to use such examinations as already existed. We had not really the organisation or the experience to promote such a scheme and it is not surprising that it failed, as A.B.C. had done, but, as we shall see later, the time is now much more propitious for the 'pilot project' approach, provided it can be launched with official support.

The universities' proposals

The first attempt by an official body to remedy the defects disclosed by Crowther was made by the Committee of Vice-Chancellors and Principals in 1962. The universities are so often accused of being the villains in this piece that it is worth remembering that they made the first concrete proposals for reform, and that these were rejected by the schools. Starting from the assumption that it was indeed university entrance requirements which were imposing on the sixth form the degree of specialisation which Crowther deplored, they proposed that the battery of 'O' and 'A' levels required for matriculation and faculty selection should be replaced by 'Course Requirements' and 'General Requirements'. As a test of course requirements, they proposed to demand two 'A' levels only in the relevant subjects and of general requirements, two general papers. The general papers were to test command of the media of communication, English, a foreign language and mathematics, with a wide range of questions on general cultural subjects.

This proposal was immediately and violently rejected by the schools on the grounds that it would favour the large well-staffed independent or direct grant schools, which could provide stimulating general courses, as compared with the small grammar school which was struggling to offer eight or nine 'A' levels. It was at this stage that one of the features which has become noticeable in this long process of frustration first appeared. The universities' proposal could have been amended to meet some of the schools' objections by structuring rather more tightly the content of the general papers. Instead the whole proposal was dropped and we returned to the slowly deteriorating *status quo*.

The Schools Council's proposals

The next episode in the story was the establishment in 1964 of the Schools Council to replace the Secondary Schools Examination Council. That a single body should concern itself both with curriculum and examinations was generally welcomed, but there was at first considerable suspicion that this was the prelude to entry by the Ministry into what the Minister then described as 'the secret garden of the curriculum'. This suspicion was gradually dissipated by a heavy representation of 'practising teachers' on the council and a studiously non-dirigiste attitude by its officers. It is arguable, in view of the difficulties we suffer from by being the only European country without some central control of the curriculum, that a bold confrontation would have suited us better. In my view, it has got to come sooner or later.

As a result, all that the Schools Council was able to do, in the matter of sixth form curriculum reform, was to provide a body which could put forward deeply considered and documented proposals for discussion. And discussion is in fact all that has happened.

The first Schools Council proposal (Working Paper no. 5, 1966) tried to give the schools what many of them had been asking for, a 'half-subject' or 'ancillary subject' in the

'A' level examination. 'A' levels were to be divided into 'major' and 'minor' subjects, so that a pattern of two majors and two minors could make up a more balanced curriculum than the three equal 'A' levels, and yet leave adequate time (assuming of course that it would be used) for unexamined general studies. A great deal of work went into preparing syllabuses and even timetables for this system, but in the end it was rejected by the schools. The reasons given for rejection seem to have been partly the same, teaching difficulties in the small sixth form, as led to the rejection of the universities' proposal, and partly concern that the new minor subjects were too like halves of 'A' level subjects, and therefore unsuitable for the 'new sixth formers' with their less academic interests.

The rejection by the representatives of the schools was decisive. The Schools Council therefore withdrew the proposal and returned in 1967 with Working Paper no. 16. This proposed that university entrance requirements should be met by two 'A' levels in the relevant subjects, the one element which remained constant in the first three official schemes, supplemented not by two minor subjects, but four to six one-year 'elective' courses, to be designed and assessed by the schools themselves, much in the manner of CSE Mode Three. This met the objectives of the schools, but it proved quite unacceptable to the universities, who foresaw that if the elective courses were to have genuine weight in the process of university selection, this would place admissions officers in the impossible situation of having to calibrate the value of an internally assessed course in industrial archaeology from a Shropshire school against that of a course in entomology from an East Anglian one. The universities at this stage began to express a preference for a pattern suggested in the Dainton Report on the Flow of Scientists and Technologists into Higher Education, which had not been worked out in any detail or discussed with the schools. This was for a sixth form course of five subjects, each

79

slightly less demanding than 'A' level, and including mathematics for all, plus one subject at least from each of the major groups of physical science, social science and humanities.

Meanwhile the Head Masters Association in *The Sixth Form of the Future* had returned to the demand for some 'level' intermediate between 'O' and 'A'.

Joint proposals: 'Q' and 'F'

In desperation, the Schools Council and the universities got together. Each set up a working party on the sixth form curriculum and university entrance. By what seemed to some people a miracle, the two working parties got together and produced a joint, unanimous recommendation. Surely now, at last, we were going to see an end to discussion and the beginning of action.

The report advocated the study of five subjects in the first year of the sixth, narrowing to three in the second. No specific recommendations were made about the distribution of the five subjects, but it was hinted that it would not come amiss if they included English, mathematics and a foreign language—the essential media of communication proposed in chapter 3 of this book. It was suggested that these five subjects should be 'by-passed' at 'O' level and tested by a 'qualifying examination' at the end of the first year of the sixth, while the three subjects carried on in the second year would be tested in a 'further examination' at the end of the course.

The proposals were immediately attacked by the schools, on the grounds that 'O' level would not in fact be by-passed (a view for which they had ample evidence as we have seen in chapter 4), and that they would therefore result in the same subject being externally examined in three successive years. Moreover, the proposal that all five subjects should be passed at the same standard in the 'qualifying examination' seemed to threaten either that the standard of that examination would be so low as to be meaningless, or that large numbers of potentially good university candidates would be excluded from higher education because they had an idiosyncratic weakness in either mathematics or a foreign language.

As in the case of the universities' proposal of 1962, these weaknesses could easily have been eliminated as a result of further dispassionate consultation. The International Baccalaureate, for instance, avoids the first by not requiring that any subject should be taken at both subsidiary and higher level and the second by the device of 'compensation', so common in Europe, by which a sub-standard performance in one of the six subjects can be retrieved by an above-standard performance in another. Instead of entering into this dialogue, however, the schools preferred to mount an impassioned campaign against 'Q' and 'F', with the result that in summer 1971, the Schools Council rejected this seventh proposal for reform and asked the two working parties to go away and think again. By the time this book is published they will presumably have come forward with their new proposal. One can only hope that it will lead to action, but the prognostications are not good. 'When the Butler-Briault joint committee produces its new sixth form proposals this summer', wrote the *Guardian* on 20 March 1972, 'there is no reason to suppose that they will not go the way of Q and F, Majors and Minors, and other half-forgotten schemes.'

The causes of stagnation

This tale of frustration raises two problems. Why is it that we are incapable of reforming our sixth form curriculum when ostensibly everyone seems agreed that it needs reform? and why is it that we enjoy such extraordinary diversity in the organisation of sixth form education, but such monolithic and unbreachable conformity in its content?

The obvious answer to the first question is that we lack any final arbiter. Unlike those of all other European countries, our central Ministry refuses to exercise any control over the curriculum. Such control as is exercised at the sixth form level rests with the autonomous examining boards. The Schools Council, the only central or representative body concerned with the curriculum, is only advisory. Consequently changes can only be introduced if every one of the 'partners' concerned, the schools, the local authorities, the examining boards and the universities are in agreement. A veto from any partner means the rejection of the proposed reform and a return to the *status quo*. So far, no proposal has been made which somebody did not object to. In all European systems, the final arbiter hears all the arguments and then decides: in ours, one black ball excludes. Some people will praise this situation as preserving the God-given right of every Englishman to do as he pleases. If everyone really agreed that reform was necessary, they will say, then surely we should have reform; and if there are those who do not want it, they should not be compelled.

What it really means, however, is the God-given right of every Englishman, in this profession, at least, to preserve the *status quo* by exercising his veto, and to prevent his colleagues from introducing changes, however much they may be in the majority and he in the minority. Although it appears on the surface that all the partners are agreed that the onset of specialisation should be postponed and its intensity diminished, there may well be many who are, unavowedly, supporters of the existing system. If so, they have only to find some argument for exercising their veto against each new proposal as it is brought forward, and they can rest assured that nothing will ever change.

The contrast with the constantly changing pattern of sixth form organisation is very marked. The reason is surely obvious. The organisation of the sixth form, in all-through comprehensives, sixth form blocks, academic colleges, junior colleges and so forth, is in the hands of the local authorities and each can experiment with whatever pattern it likes. The curriculum of the sixth form is in the hands of the examining boards and the university admissions officers and they are obsessed with uniformity and comparability. All universities measure their entry requirements in 'A' and 'O' levels and all boards provide 'A' and 'O' levels as nearly as they can in the same subjects and at the same levels.

The case for a pilot scheme

If there is little chance of finding a general pattern of curriculum reform which is not displeasing to anybody, and which all parties would agree to implement on a national scale as quickly as possible, is there any hope that we may be allowed to learn in this area, as we are learning in the area of sixth form organisation, through a number of small-scale experiments? If we can have five combined sixth forms and colleges of further education, could we not have had five schools trying out a modified 'Q' and 'F'?

This device of experimental Baccalaureates or *Lycées pilotes* is not unknown in Europe. It is perhaps unreasonable to hope that a new system can be found which is approved by everyone—certainly the existing system is not—but why must we assume that we must either all move together or all stand still together?

The first proposal which we put forward from Oxford in 1960 was that a group of schools should band together to try out a broader curriculum. It came to nothing because at that stage we had only the existing 'A' levels to use and because we had no machinery for ensuring that the universities would accept our candidates. We have now the International Baccalaureate, which I would defend as an improved version of 'Q' and 'F', and which every university in England and Wales has agreed to accept on an experimental basis as an entry qualification. In March 1970 a group of representatives from schools met and agreed to work on a plan for a pilot experiment, using this examination instead of 'A' level, *provided* that the Schools Council would support it as a nationally recognised pilot scheme. Nothing came of it because everybody seems too busy trying to find a nationally agreed solution applicable across the board.

Nothing but a pilot scheme of this sort can provide the evidence on which the perennial questions about 'adequate preparation for university entry in the specialist subjects' or 'the necessity of four year university courses' (because the subject has been studied for one hour a week less at school) or 'the negation of subject-mindedness' can be realistically judged. Such a pilot scheme is now possible, but only if it has official backing. After all, though it may be true that the universities would accept such a scheme based on the International Baccalaureate, less than half the sixth form are going to universities, and the rest would need some official validation of their diplomas and partial certificates. Nevertheless, it could be done if we had the will to do it. If the next attempt at a universal reform goes the same way as the last seven attempts, is it too much to hope that we might try the effect of that freedom to experiment in the curriculum which sixth forms at present enjoy in organisation?

Finally, then, what sort of a sixth form might we hope to see emerge from such a pattern of experiment?

It must be one which stretches and develops the full powers of the mind, both intellectually and operationally, while not neglecting the stimulation and refinement of moral and aesthetic sensitivity, as expressed not merely in passive awareness but in action and creation. At the same time, it must attract, as it surely would if it met these criteria, a much higher proportion of the age group to remain in full-time education. It must so teach that pupils

84

develop a continuing desire for life-long education and an acquaintance with the methods by which they may pursue it. In its organisation it must be so designed as not to polarise the young into 'intellectual' and 'anti-intellectual' factions more than necessary and to make the most economic use of scarce resources, including the scarcest of all, outstanding teachers.

There is much to be done, and much that will involve changes unwelcome to somebody, before we can claim to be even approaching these objectives.

Bibliography

It is normal in this series to provide 'suggestions for further reading', but little has in fact been written on the specific topic of this book. I have preferred, therefore, to provide an annotated bibliography.

BLOOM, J. S., *Taxonomy of Educational Objectives*, Longmans (1965). The classic statement of the need to define in operational terms the objectives of educational procedures if the success or failure of such procedures is to be evaluated. It includes a very detailed scheme for the classification of objectives.

CENTRAL ADVISORY COUNCIL FOR EDUCATION (England), *Early Leaving*, HMSO (1954). A Ministry of Education report which disclosed the high proportion of those selected for entry to grammar schools who failed to complete the course. Now mainly of historic interest.

CENTRAL ADVISORY COUNCIL FOR EDUCATION (England), *Fifteen to Eighteen* (Crowther Report), HMSO (1959). The official report on which most subsequent discussion was based. It introduced such terms as 'subject-mindedness', 'minority time', 'literacy and numeracy'. The statistical appendices are now of historic interest.

DEPARTMENT OF EDUCATION AND SCIENCE, *Teacher Educa-*

tion and Training (James Report), HMSO (1972). The sections on the nature of the proposed Diploma in Higher Education are relevant to consideration of general education in the sixth form.

EDWARDS, A. D., *The Changing Sixth Form in the Twentieth Century*, Routledge & Kegan Paul (1970). Essential historical background to consideration of the present state of the sixth form.

GOODMAN, P., *Compulsory Miseducation*, Horizon Publishers (1962). An early American attack on the irrelevance of much traditional teaching of school subjects.

HEAD MASTERS ASSOCIATION, *The Sixth Form of the Future* (1968). An analysis by the Head Masters Association of the problems of the new sixth form. Its proposals for reform deserve consideration along with those of the universities and of the Schools Council.

ILIFFE, A. H., *The Foundation Year at Keele*, University of Keele (1966). Report of research on the sixth form education of undergraduates entering the University of Keele.

ILLICH, I., *De-schooling Society*, Calder & Boyars (1971). The most celebrated of many attacks on conventional schooling in the USA.

INNER LONDON EDUCATION AUTHORITY, *Sixth Form Opportunities in Inner London*, ILEA (1968). A factual report on a single, but very important, area.

MCGRATH, E. J., *Universal Higher Education*, McGraw-Hill (1966). An interesting, although already dated, symposium on the implications of expanding educational opportunity.

MICHAEL, D. P. M., *Guide to the Sixth Form*, Pergamon Press (1969). A practical guide to success in the existing sixth form curriculum and examinations.

MUMFORD, D., *Comprehensive Reorganisation in the Junior College*, ACFHE (1970). A plea for the integration of sixth form and college of education by the Principal of the Cambridgeshire College of Arts and Technology.

NEWSOM, D., *Godliness and Good Learning*, Murray (1962).

A historic survey of the values and objectives of sixth form teaching in the nineteenth century.

OECD, *Development in Secondary Education* (1969). An international survey of secondary education in Europe.

OXFORD UNIVERSITY DEPARTMENT OF EDUCATION, *Arts and Science Sides in the Sixth Form* (1960). Report of the first research project on patterns of sixth form curriculum and student preferences. Out of print but available in many college libraries.

PETERSON, A. D. C., *The Future of Education*, Cresset Press (1968). An essay in futurology applied to the comparatively immediate future of education in this country.

PETERSON, A. D. C., *The International Baccalaureate*, Harrap (1972). A description of the new sixth form programmes and examinations developed in international schools.

POLANYI, M., *Personal Knowledge*, Routledge & Kegan Paul (1962). A philosopher's account of the nature of knowledge. Perhaps a useful counter-balance to many accepted theories.

SCHOOLS COUNCIL, *Sixth Form Pupils and Teachers* (1970). The only really exhaustive treatment of the existing situation.

TAYLOR, L. C., *Resources for Learning*, Penguin (1971). This very useful discussion of teaching method also contains a valuable analysis of the changes in the nature of the sixth form which call for new teaching methods.